THE CO-VANS

THE CO-VANS

U.S. Marine Advisors in Vietnam

JOHN GRIDER MILLER

Naval Institute Press

Annapolis, Maryland

Naval Institute Press
291 Wood Road
Annapolis, MD 21402

Library of Congress Cataloging-in-Publication Data
Miller, John Grider, 1935–
The co-vans : U.S. Marine advisors in Vietnam / John Grider Miller.
    p. cm.
ISBN 1-55750-549-7 (alk. paper)
    1. Vietnamese Conflict, 1961–1975—Personal narratives, Ameri-
can. 2. Miller, John Grider, 1935– I. Title.

DS559.5 .M55 2000
959.704'3'092—dc21
                                                    00-0033922

Printed in the United States of America on acid-free paper ∞
07 06 05 04 03 02 01 00   9 8 7 6 5 4 3 2
First printing

While large U.S. Marine Corps forces were operating in Vietnam, co-vans, or advisors, to the Vietnamese Marine Corps (VNMC) were well out of the mainstream, laboring in isolation and obscurity in what was perceived as a backwater. Yet there were always more than enough volunteers ready to be advisors even though such duty was neither required nor expected of them. Indeed, prospective co-vans needed a certain measure of pull to get into the Marine Advisory Unit. Each volunteer had his own reason for signing on, but—at the heart of things—almost every volunteer had proven himself to be a fighter before becoming an advisor. And the advisory effort got the best. The Marine advisors were an elite serving with an elite. It is no coincidence that much of the top-rung leadership during Operations Desert Shield and Desert Storm in 1990–91 were former Marine co-vans, including Generals Boomer, Myatt, Keys, Sheehan, Hopkins, Neal, and Brabham.

The tour in John Grider Miller's career that has left the deepest mark on him was serving outside the cocoon of the Marine Corps itself as an advisor to the Vietnamese Marines. He writes proudly of that experience in *The Co-Vans*, most often with a light and irreverently humorous touch, but sometimes also with a tinge of bitterness at what was and what might have been. He believes that in the final analysis the Vietnam War was an Asian war—a continuation of conflicts fought for centuries. His unmistakable conclusion is that, in retrospect, the East remains inscrutably East and West is irrevocably West—so perhaps Rudyard Kipling had it right.

The original Vietnamese term, *cố-vấn,* translates simply into "trusted friend" and was applied to Army and Navy advisors as well as Marines. A co-van soon learned that the last thing his Vietnamese "counterpart" needed or wanted was advice on how to fight the Vietcong and North Vietnamese Army. What Vietnamese commanders and staff officers at all levels did need was strong linkage to powerful U.S. tactical and logistical support systems.

For a Marine advisor it was a lonely business. He was serving apart from any major U.S. force, and this sense of isolation deepened when his Vietnamese unit went into the field. With only one or two advisors assigned to battalions that often split in two parts for operations, the co-van did without either casual or meaningful conversation unless he was truly fluent—and few of the advisors were—in the difficult Vietnamese language. He was very much alone but, paradoxically, as one American among hundreds of Vietnamese, he lived in a veritable fishbowl, with every action being watched by someone, ranging from his radio operator to his battalion-commander counterpart.

John Miller joined the Vietnamese Marines in early 1970, in time for its brigade-sized operations in the Cambodian incursion, followed by operations in the Middle Region southwest of Da Nang. Then came Lam Son 719, the long-anticipated march out Route 9 into Laos in 1971—the largest South Vietnamese-run offensive of the war. In essence, the problems confronting the Vietnamese Marines and their advisors in this, the stiffest challenge faced up to that time, differed little except in magnitude from problems endemic ever since VNMC's inception fifteen years earlier.

After the defeat of the French by the Viet Minh at Dien Bien Phu in 1954, the Indo-China War had moved swiftly to its ambiguous conclusion. In what was to have been a temporary partition, Vietnam was divided, the North from the South, along a line a bit north of the ancient imperial city of Hue. In the sorting out of the opposing forces, the remnants of northern-based elements of the Vietnamese National Army moved to the south. This included a collection of commando-type units.

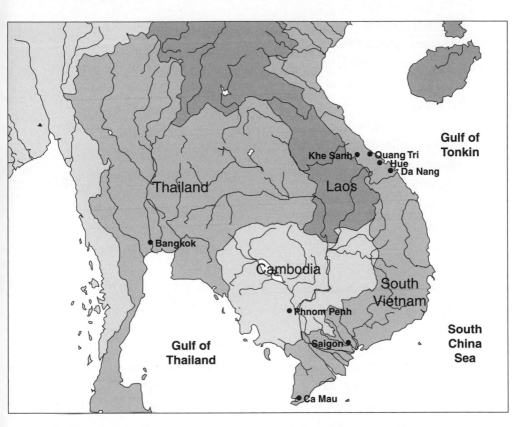

Southeast Asia

These had operated in the Red River Delta with the French and Vietnamese Navy river assault division called *dinassauts,* each of which was composed of a dozen or so command vessels, patrol boats, and armored landing craft carrying a hundred-man commando unit. These commando units, specially trained by the French for duty with the *dinassauts,* were variously designated as light support companies, riverboat companies, and commandos. Collectively, although they were never so named, they formed a rudimentary riverine marine corps.

By early 1955 a total of 2,400 officers and men from these landing parties had been relocated in South Vietnam, for the most part at Nha Trang, a one-time seaside resort on the China Sea, where the French still maintained an extensive naval training facility. Several of the commandos were collected into the First (Marine) Landing Battalion under the command of Capt. Jean Louis Delayen, a combat-wise French commando officer. The remainder—including six riverboat companies and five light combat support companies—were scattered about in small, widely separated garrisons between Hue City in the north and the Mekong Delta in the south. Ngo Dinh Diem, by then South Vietnam's premier, appointed an Army officer, Maj. Le Quang Trong, as the senior officer of the fledgling Vietnamese Marine Corps. Lacking a headquarters and a command structure, Trong could exercise little control over his widely scattered troops.

At this point, Lt. Col. Victor J. Croizat, USMC, born in North Africa and fluent in French, entered the scene. At Guadalcanal he had been a pioneer in the use of amphibian tractors. He originally was ordered to Vietnam to be a liaison officer with the French High Command. But when he arrived in August 1954, the cease-fire agreement between the French and the Viet Minh already had been signed and the liaison billet no longer existed. He was reassigned to the newly created General Commission for Refugees. After working in South Vietnam to develop refugee reception centers and resettlement areas, he traveled north to the port city of Haiphong, where until February 1955 he headed the U.S. Military Assistance Advisory Group detachment that coordinated the "Passage to Freedom" refugee-evacuation operation. Despite uncertainties surrounding the new government under the figurehead Emperor Bao Dai, nearly a million refugees, a large percentage of them Catholic, eventually moved through a French-controlled corridor between Hanoi and Haiphong for seaborne evacuation to South Vietnam.

Croizat returned to Saigon to become the senior U.S. advisor to the Vietnamese Marine Corps, newly created by formal decree, but loosely organized and with an uncertain future. Even as the French presence in Vietnam receded, the scattered Vietnamese Marine units continued to be dependent upon the French Expeditionary Force for logistical support. In Saigon, the South Vietnamese Army, Navy, and Air Force had seasoned senior officers, their own as well as French and American, to advance their respective causes. There was no such reservoir of experience for the Vietnamese Marines.

The relatively junior Croizat was left to wonder about the impact his advice could have, funneled as it would be through a Franco-American training mission. He knew that the French, because of the concentrations of people and economic activity along the rivers and coastline, were strong believers in a coastal and riverine navy for South Vietnam. The development of such a navy could be reasonably foreseen. There were no such guarantees of support for a complementary corps of marines, especially in light of the Vietnamese Army's ceaseless efforts to gain control of all facets of ground combat. In a situation analogous to the experience of the United States Marines, the development of a Vietnamese Army, Navy, and Air Force was assured, but the Vietnamese Marines themselves would have to prove that there should also be a Vietnamese Marine Corps.

An opportunity to do so was not long in coming. In February 1955, the leaders of the Hoa Hao, Cao Dai, and Binh Xuyen sects formed a United Front of National Forces. Premier Diem refused to accede to their demands for what amounted to autonomy. The Hoa Hao began guerrilla actions in March, and Diem's battalions, including the First Marine Landing Battalion, struck back. The Marines won a notable battle with the Hoa Hao in Kien Giang Province and—shortly before the sect movement collapsed entirely—carried the fight against the Binh Xuyen into the swampy Rung Sat Special Zone just south of Saigon.

Weathering this crisis with the sects enabled Diem to sidestep a transparent attempt by Emperor Bao Dai to remove him from office. Bao Dai was himself riding out the crisis in France. Diem refused to obey the

Emperor's summons to join him for "consultations," and on 23 October 1955 he won a nationwide referendum that made him the first president of the new Republic of Vietnam.

Prior to his employment of the First Marine Landing Battalion against the sects, Diem had replaced Captain Delayen with Capt. Bui Phu Chi, a small part of the process of substituting Vietnamese officers for French throughout his armed forces. Captain Delayen stayed on at Nha Trang as the battalion's advisor until his place was taken by Captain James T. Breckinridge in 1955. This started the chain of U.S. Marine advisors at the operational level.

Meanwhile Lieutenant Colonel Croizat had established a goal of a three-battalion Vietnamese Marine regiment. Before he left in 1956 he had the satisfaction of seeing the old riverboat and light support companies consolidated into a second landing battalion, and the organization of a 4.2-inch mortar company and a regimental headquarters and service company. He left behind a staff study that called for the transfer of a Vietnamese Army amphibious battalion to the Marines, to give the regiment its third battalion and still stay within the overall personnel ceiling authorized for the South Vietnamese armed forces. Three years passed before this recommendation was implemented.

Indeed, shortly after Croizat's departure, the minister of defense made a bold attempt to incorporate the Vietnamese Marines into the Army of the Republic of Vietnam. Only the high regard Diem had for the combat exploits of the Marine Landing Battalion saved the Vietnamese Marine Corps from extinction. This pattern of recommended absorption into the Army would recycle repeatedly for the next two decades—the life span of the Republic of Vietnam. The U.S. Marine advisors would come to recognize episodes in this pattern with a certain weary sense of déjà vu.

The co-vans, moving through these uncertain years and seeing their counterparts faced with the need to be on guard against all potential enemies—foreign and domestic—developed a pervasive independence of spirit and thought. To outsiders, the co-vans sometimes appeared paranoid or at least arrogant. But the advisors preached to themselves that aggressiveness and mental toughness were survival tools in an alien world where nothing could be taken for granted. Even their own acceptance by the Vietnamese Marines could not be guaranteed. The testing of a new advisor began on the day of his arrival and it would continue until he proved himself.

Such isolated duty with foreign military units was nothing particularly new, in one form or another, for the U.S. Marines. In the so-called Banana Wars during the first half of the twentieth century in the Caribbean, U.S. Marines had served as officers in the *guardias* of Santo Domingo and Nicaragua and the *gendarmerie* of Haiti. In World War II, Marines served as advisors with Chinese Nationalist guerrillas and later with Republic of China Marines on Taiwan. In Korea they were with the Republic of Korea Marine Corps. At the spectacular peak of co-van activity in Vietnam—the 1972 Easter Offensive—U.S. Marine advisors were also assisting sixteen other Marine Corps–related entities scattered around the globe. In some parts of the world such service continues, in one guise or another.

The U.S. Army approach to advisory duty differed markedly from the U.S. Marine approach. The Army preferred to work in teams, setting up, as the Marine co-vans saw it, Little Americas in the midst of command posts down to the battalion level. An underlying U.S. Army reason for the team approach was to give each team a last-ditch self-defense capability in the event that they were abandoned by their Vietnamese counterparts. A generally held Marine view was that the Army method created an unnecessary "we-they" split that made impossible any true rapport between a co-van and his Vietnamese counterpart or "buddy." So who was right?

Most Marine co-vans believed that the Team America concept stopped short of a total commitment and made it easier for some U.S. Army advisors to separate from their Vietnamese units *in extremis.* Further, no Marine advisor ever died because he stuck with his Vietnamese counterpart to the bitter end—although there were some chillingly close calls. Unlike the Army's self-defense approach, the Marine advisors believed, rather pragmatically, that no enemy attacking force powerful enough to fight its way through a battalion of Vietnamese Marines would be slowed down for very long by a handful of Americans. No matter who was right, these differences in organization and philosophy sometimes caused a coolness between U.S. Army and U.S. Marine advisors, just as there were often strained relations between the Army of the Republic of Vietnam

(ARVN) and the Vietnamese Marine Corps. But the record of the war also is replete with examples of the ARVN and Vietnamese Marines fighting heroically side by side, giving each other a full measure of support.

The total-immersion approach to advisory duty generally made sense to the U.S. Marines but it was no guarantee of continuous smooth sailing, either in the field or in garrison. As this volume amply demonstrates, stark cultural differences—embodied in the concept of "Face," in the "Commander Syndrome," and in less lofty manifestations—never could be swept aside entirely. The advisors had to become adept in getting around these problems.

John Grider Miller—the "Grider" is important, as it distinguishes him from all the other "John Millers" in the world—was born in the Annapolis Emergency Hospital on 23 August 1935. The influence of Annapolis upon him has been large ever since. His father, John Stanley Miller, was U.S. Naval Academy, Class of 1932. One of his father's roommates at the Academy was John McGavock Grider, a life-long friend, hence the "Grider" in John's name.

John grew up in the Virginia and Maryland suburbs of Washington, D.C. He attended Bethesda–Chevy Chase High School with every hope and expectation of going to the Naval Academy. In his senior year, he had a narrow miss at getting an appointment, but competed successfully for a Naval Reserve Officers Training Corps regular scholarship and was accepted by Yale University, the college of his choice. On his second-summer midshipman cruise at the amphibious base at Little Creek, Virginia, he decided he wanted to be a Marine.

He was commissioned on graduation in June 1957. His first years as a lieutenant—after attending the Basic School at Quantico, the Marine Corps's great leveler for newly commissioned officers—were spent in a mixture of troop-leading and staff assignments in infantry battalions at Camp Pendleton and on Okinawa. On his return to the States, he was picked to go to Marine Barracks, Washington, in May 1961. With its evening parades, burial details with full honors, and White House assignments, the barracks at Eighth and Eye Streets, S.E., was and is the ceremonial heart of the Marine Corps.

As a captain, he had his tactical skills tuned up by attendance at U.S. Army infantry and airborne schools at Fort Benning in 1964–65. He reported to Camp Pendleton in time to sail with the First Battalion, First Marines, for South Vietnam. Working out of the combat bases at Da Nang, Phu Bai, and Khe Sanh, he commanded Company D, First Battalion, and later was the battalion assistant operations officer.

Returning to the United States in 1966, he was assigned to CinCLant headquarters at Norfolk as aide and executive assistant to the Deputy Chief of Staff, at first Maj. Gen. Sidney S. Wade, who had commanded the Marines in the 1958 Lebanon intervention, and then Maj. Gen. John H. "Bud" Masters, an extremely well-liked officer who became John's role model. After three years at CinCLant, with a promotion to major, John was ordered to the Armed Forces Staff College. From here, he was selected to serve as an advisor.

He came home in 1971 and, promoted to lieutenant colonel, spent a long spell as a speech writer for successive Marine Corps commandants, Generals Chapman, Cushman, and Wilson. He attended the Naval War College at Newport in 1976–77 and then returned to troop duty at Camp Lejeune and in the Mediterranean. He served first as executive officer of the Eighth Marine Regiment, then as commanding officer of the First Battalion, Eighth Marines, and later of its expeditionary alternative, Battalion Landing Team 1/8. Following this he was exec of Marine Amphibious Unit 22.

He came back to Headquarters, Marine Corps, in 1979 to be the executive assistant to Maj. Gen. Edward J. Megarr, the Director of Operations and Training. Next, he became the head of the Amphibious Requirements Branch, where his main projects were bringing in and monitoring the air-cushion landing craft (LCAC) and landing dock ship (LSD-41) programs.

There was one more overseas tour. He went to Okinawa in June 1982 to be G-3 (Operations and Plans) of the III Marine Amphibious Force. A year later he returned to Headquarters, Marine Corps, for the last time and for service as Deputy Director of Marine Corps History. His chief focus in that billet, as my deputy, was bringing out the official histories of U.S. Marine operations in Vietnam.

He retired as a colonel in 1985 and went back to his birthplace, Annapolis, to be the managing editor of the U.S. Naval Institute's two magazines, the venerable *Proceedings* and the new *Naval History,* which he helped establish. *The Co-Vans* is his fourth book. The others are *The Battle to Save the Houston* (1985) and *The Bridge at Dong Ha* (1989), both published by the U.S. Naval Institute Press, and *Punching Out: Launching a Post-Military Career* (1994), St. Martin's Press.

EDWIN HOWARD SIMMONS

Brigadier General, U.S. Marine Corps (Retired)

Director Emeritus, Marine Corps History

ACKNOWLEDGMENTS

The list is small, but my gratitude is immense:

To former Naval Institute Press acquisitions editor Scott Belliveau, whose early encouragement and support brought the project to life;

To my former Senior Marine Advisor Frank Tief and former Assistant Senior Marine Advisor Pat McMillan, both retired general officers, whose thorough review brought valuable additions and corrections to the draft manuscript;

To my former assistant G-3 advisor Marsh Carter, who provided equally valuable input and has shown by example that co-vans can become major bank presidents as well as general officers;

To Marine Corps Chief Historian Chuck Melson, who provided archival documents, including some of my own long-forgotten notes, to fill the memory gaps that tend to develop over a period of nearly three decades;

To my good friend Jack Maxwell, who, based on my assurances that the various statutes of limitation probably had run their course, permitted some of his bigger-than-life deeds and misdeeds to be recorded for posterity; and

To my dear wife Susan, for enduring yet another spell as a "book widow," but being willing once again to use her computer skills to direct my manuscript toward the Naval Institute Press and not down our home computer's memory hole.

A final acknowledgement must go to the men who wore the tiger suits, and the co-vans who valiantly carried on the fight in a war that most of their countrymen were trying desperately to forget. It was their finest hour.

In 1968, Richard M. Nixon, pledging to bring peace with honor to war-ravaged Vietnam, was elected president of the United States. Large-scale troop withdrawals soon began, on a timetable that seemed rushed to some at first, but only accelerated as time went on.

With the emergence and implementation of a policy of "Vietnamization"—gradually turning the war over to the South Vietnamese armed forces—there was some danger of the conflict being Vietnamized too rapidly. Left holding the bag too soon, underprepared Vietnamese forces might not even be able to cover the withdrawal of U.S. units, much less defend their own country for very long. "Peace with honor" would carry a bitter, mocking resonance through the ages if the carefully planned withdrawal were to disintegrate into a collapse, and then into a military rout.

Concerned by a steady buildup of supplies and equipment in communist base areas just beyond South Vietnam's borders in Laos and Cambodia—fourteen hitherto untouchable sanctuaries—U.S. and Vietnamese planners had contemplated a ground attack into Cambodia since the spring of 1969. Politically, it would have been preferable to make this an all-Vietnamese operation; militarily, a strong U.S. presence on the ground would be mandatory to make it work, even if defensive strong points and heavily populated areas were bypassed. Finally, in the spring of 1970, the White House approved a limited U.S.-Vietnamese incursion into

Cambodia. American troops could advance no deeper than twenty-five miles beyond the border, and would have to return to South Vietnam within two months. It would be the largest operation of the war, involving some 30,000 Vietnamese and 20,000 U.S. troops. As preparations for the attack commenced, the allies looked for a favorable time to launch.

An opportunity did not take long to arrive. In March 1970, while Cambodia's Prince Norodom Sihanouk was traveling outside the country, the National Assembly replaced him with the pro-American General Lon Nol. Prime Minister Sihanouk, who had been proclaiming Cambodia's neutrality while allowing the North Vietnamese unfettered use of border sanctuaries, might have made an allied cross-border operation quite difficult in a political sense, both in the United States and in the eyes of the world. Lon Nol, on the other hand, was likely to view any dislodgment of North Vietnamese stationed in his country as good riddance.

On 29 April 1970, the Army of the Republic of Viet Nam (ARVN) forces attacked into two of Cambodia's most significant border sanctuaries, known as Parrot's Beak and Fishhook. Two days later, the first U.S. and additional ARVN units drove into more base areas. The initial results were spectacular; North Vietnamese defenders followed instructions to conserve their forces by withdrawing westward, thus abandoning more than 9,000 tons of supplies, weapons, and ammunition and another 7,000 tons of rice—enough to feed and supply all their forces in South Vietnam for at least six months.

In the United States the initial reaction also was spectacular, as antiwar activists began to scream about widening the war, glossing over the fact that the base areas were manned not by neutral Cambodians but by North Vietnamese soldiers placed there to support other North Vietnamese soldiers who were attacking South Vietnam. Protests erupted; college campuses found themselves in turmoil; and several closed their doors after four students died at Kent State.

In June, the Senate passed the Cooper-Church amendment to a military appropriations bill, which would have withheld funding for any U.S. ground troops, advisors, or air support in Cambodia. The initial amendment died in the House of Representatives. A weakened version, which still prohibited ground troops in either Cambodia or Laos but continued support for the Lon Nol government, passed both houses in December. This was six months too late to have any impact upon U.S. troops in Cambodia, because they had returned to South Vietnam by the end of June, on Nixon's orders. Nevertheless, that amendment passed just in time to limit U.S. support for Operation Lam Son 719, a 1971 cross-border foray into Laos to cut the Ho Chi Minh Trail.

The Vietnamese Marines received their warning order for the Cambodian incursion, code-named Operation Tran Hung Dao IX, on the evening of 6 May 1970. Within twelve hours, Brigade B (consisting of the First, Fourth, and Fifth Infantry Battalions and a battery from the Second Artillery Battalion) was embarked on the landing craft of Amphibious Task Force 211 and moving northward along the Mekong River. Roughly fifteen miles inside Cambodia, the First Battalion ran into heavy resistance from a suspected North Vietnamese Army (NVA) regional headquarters area on the east bank of the Mekong. As the Marines stormed ashore, the artillery battery was landed on a nearby island and went into action quickly to provide indirect fire support in a swift victory.

Meanwhile, the rest of Brigade B continued moving toward the ferry-crossing site at Neak Luong, astride the road to the capital city of Phnom Penh. While the Fifth Battalion landed and cleared enemy forces from the east bank, the Fourth Battalion wrapped things up on the western side of the river. Two sharp actions were fought with advisor support, south of the twenty-five-mile limit of advance for U.S. personnel, on 14 and 20 May. On 28 May, Brigade A (consisting of the Second, Sixth, Seventh, and Eighth Infantry Battalions and most of the Second Artillery Battalion) replaced Brigade B at Neak Luong, without missing a beat. Almost immediately, the Second Battalion made a Vietnamese Air Force–supported heliborne assault into the provincial capital town of Prey Veng. In the ensuing six-day fight, the Second Battalion, reinforced by the Fourth Battalion and receiving VNAF air support, cleared the town in vicious house-to-house fighting.

Two aspects of this victory were particularly noteworthy: Skillful use of Marine artillery, swiftly displaced by landing craft to new firing positions, had a devastating effect on the NVA forces yet spared the town from heavy damage. And because Prey Veng was north of the twenty-five-mile limit, the action there was conducted without the direct presence of co-vans at battalion level—a most unusual state of affairs, but one in which the Vietnamese Marines acquitted themselves marvelously.

It was a harbinger of good things—and bad things—to come.

Chapter **I**

Maj. Ted Gatchel was the happiest man I'd ever seen.

Ted was waiting for me to relieve him as the senior *cố-vấn* of the South Vietnamese Marines' Brigade A, then two months into their 1970 cross-border thrust into Cambodia. As my helicopter hovered over the landing pad at Neak Luong and began its final descent, the prop wash plastered Ted's paper-thin tiger suit—with its distinctive spiky jungle-camouflage markings now faded and blurred—against his gaunt body. After a year as a "co-van," Ted was going home, and he was glowing. Ever the gentleman, he tried not to be too obvious about it.

After four months of schoolwork, training, travel, and briefings, I was ready to begin earning my pay as a co-van. Just days before, I had arrived in South Vietnam on a Flying Tigers chartered airline—a far cry from my arrival five years earlier, on a beat-up troopship. Back then, as we approached Da Nang, our Marines receiving weapons instruction on the ship's fantail could see air strikes being put into the distant hills. This time, as we crossed the coastline of Vietnam at thirty thousand feet, I could see a severe firefight directly below—with the red outgoing tracers (ours) and the green incoming tracers (theirs) moving across the darkened landscape. Most likely, we were flying over the Rung Sat Special Zone, that swampy hellhole near Saigon. A flight attendant offered me a foil-wrapped grilled cheese sandwich. Why not indulge? I would be out of the box seats and onto the field soon enough.

The flight landed at Saigon's Tan Son Nhut airport in the middle of the night. Even past midnight, the terminal was sweaty, noisy, and crowded with people on their way to new futures—in Saigon or elsewhere. Half were arriving; the other more boisterous half were headed back to the States—the Land of the Big PX—with unadulterated joy that few took pains to conceal. Long lines were forming for everything, and it looked like a long morning ahead until a co-van in a tiger suit and green beret magically emerged from the turmoil and guided me skillfully through the check-in procedures, bypassing the lines and the red tape. For a moment, I felt like a Very Important Person instead of a weary, almost-invisible traveler half a world away from home. All I needed to complete the illusion would be a stretch limousine and a police escort; instead, my seabag and I soon were perched in the back of the co-van's jeep, speeding through the dark and deserted Saigon streets toward the Splendid Hotel, in the center of town.

Requisitioned as a military bachelor officers' quarters, the Splendid was anything but. Nevertheless, it would be home—at least until I went to the field. And even while I was in the field, my Saigon-based roommate would provide a daily watch on personal gear left behind in the hotel.

The next day, at the Marine Headquarters—the Bộ Tư Lệnh—they wasted no time in getting me ready to go into Cambodia. They measured me for uniforms and briefed me on the sixteen-year history of the South Vietnamese Marines, direct descendants of the French-led river assault groups in the earlier war up north against the Viet Minh. Finally, they briefed me on the current situation in Cambodia.

By the end of the second day, I had received six sets of tailor-made tiger suits, complete with embroidered nametags and jump wings. This was the uniform for both the field (with a camouflaged cover) and on liberty in town, with a green beret. The beret was not the U.S. type, perched on the head like a lean-to, but a more natural French one, which could be rolled and stowed under a shoulder strap then magically resume its proper shape when the time came to wear it again. The distinctive jungle-camouflage cloth for these uniforms came from South Korea. It was lightweight but strong, and it let your skin breathe. You could wade across a stream and

At the not-so-splendid entrance to the Hotel Splendid, white fifty-five-gallon drums filled with sand are placed to prevent Vietcong passing on motor bikes from rolling hand grenades into the lobby. The sign on the black drum advises the occupants to clear their sidearms before entering the hotel.

walk yourself dry within a half-hour. I immediately put two tiger suits into the laundry, to wash away the newness before I took them into Cambodia. It would take many washings, over many months, to attain the faded look of the long-service co-vans.

Within a week, I had been fully briefed at all the major U.S. and Vietnamese headquarters and was ready to go. The helicopter flight from Saigon to the Cambodian river-crossing site at Neak Luong, on the east bank of the Mekong, was short, less than two hours. The turnover conference with the glowing Ted Gatchel was mercifully brief. He handed me his packet of maps. I already knew the Big Picture, and other co-vans on the scene could fill in the little picture. Furthermore, the helicopter that brought me to Cambodia was turning and burning on the pad, waiting impatiently to get Ted Gatchel back to Saigon before dark. So, if there were no more questions. . . ?

The happy afterglow of Ted's departure dissipated along with the dust that swirled, then settled after the helicopter lifted off. I would not be able to meet my counterpart, the brigade commander, until the following morning, so it was time to settle in. Another co-van brought forward my cowboy—an enlisted batman, along the lines of the British model—who helped carry my gear over to the place that housed the co-vans. An undistinguished dwelling in a shaded residential area on the outskirts of town, the house had a big back porch with its own personal flying bat, which delighted in streaking at low altitude from one end to the other, daring anyone to swat it with a rolled-up newspaper.

After staking out a cot on the back porch, I took up the next burning issue of the day—dinner—with my cowboy. After a week of Western meals at the Splendid and various Americanized nightspots in Saigon, I was ready to go Vietnamese; maybe chicken tonight, okay? The cowboy replied with some consternation that he could go into town and buy a *gà,* but it probably would cost *beaucoup*. And besides, there was a stockpile of C-rations in the brigade command post. They were easier to prepare and didn't cost anything and that's what the other nearby co-vans were eating. They considered C-rations a welcome change from rice-and-roots in the field.

Even though the Oriental concept of saving and losing face was still imperfectly developed inside my own brain housing group, something told me that it would be unwise to let my cowboy back me down the very first time I asked him to do anything. So I informed him politely that I had decided on a ga dinner, so he'd best go into town and find me a succulent *gà* for dinner.

When the tasty ga dinner was served a couple of hours later, I began to sense the immensity of my error. After a quick look at the plate, I immediately understood that, while Ted Gatchel's cowboy may have failed in his mission to fatten him up, mine was not even going to try. As a New Guy I had been assigned a distinctly low-cuisine cowboy, and until I had proven myself worthy in combat, I could bloody well starve. Later on, there would be small but distinct improvements in my standard of living if I passed the test.

In any case, it was evident that I had not arrived yet. The scrawny chicken had indeed cost far more per pound than a choice Porterhouse steak, and my cowboy had proved to be a ga-cooker of the boil-and-dice school. The pale, unappetizing bird had been chopped into tiny bits, with flesh and bones all mixed together. After the first two bites, I was uncomfortably full, but pressed on gamely. The cowboy asked if he could have the feet—not the legs, the feet—and I acquiesced, then watched in near horror as he boiled them for a while, then stripped off the yellowish skin with his teeth, then ate it. There must have been tiny fat pockets in the skin that made it a delicacy. At any rate, the cowboy stopped short of doing anything with the greyish leg bones under the skin. Everyone has his limits, I guess.

As I attempted to walk off this first Vietnamese/Cambodian dinner, en route to the advisors' back porch, I was hailed by a Vietnamese major whom I recognized as the brigade's operations officer. He was sitting on a balcony of a distinctly more sumptuous house than the co-vans occupied, and waved me up to share an after-dinner drink—or so I thought. I soon was to learn that the Vietnamese considered drinking without food being served to be a barbaric (albeit distinctly American) custom, when his cowboy brought out a bowl of nicely browned chicken parts (un-diced) that would have made a hit at any Stateside bar's happy hour. It was enough to make me forget my dinnertime disaster—for a few brief moments, anyway—as I accepted the major's offer of food and drink. After we exchanged pleasantries, the major, quite fluent in English, took charge of the conversation. Within minutes, I was beginning to see an entirely new dimension of life in the Vietnamese Marines and Brigade A, far beyond the insights gained through any formal briefings.

After a half-hour, I was uncomfortably full again and ready to leave, but the major was just getting warmed up, and the food and drink kept coming. Maybe this was the way the major ate his dinner. After an hour, I was in real pain, but my newfound friend was still going strong and I didn't want to shut him off by appearing to reject his hospitality. Finally, as sundown drew near, the major slowed down. Then the food stopped arriving. Then we were finishing our final drink and bidding a cheery adieu, and I was stumbling through the dark toward my back porch, convinced that I would not need to eat again for a week. Not even our back-porch bat, gearing up for the night's activities, could bother me as I found my cot and crashed with no more disrobing than loosening my belt.

One fleeting thought crossed my mind as I drifted off. How on earth did Ted Gatchel get to be so gaunt?

Awakened by a pair of competing roosters at daybreak, I felt much better. I poured water from a five-gallon can into my helmet and took it over to a jeep where I could shave, using a side mirror. Then I pulled out a small pouch with the components of my portable double-edge razor, for its first use in the field. The parts screwed together easily, and after a couple of blade swipes, I took my first look in the jeep mirror. The lower part of my face was covered in blood from two scrapes along my cheekbones, and a crowd of Cambodians was gathering—chattering and pointing. Carrying the parts around loose must have knocked the razor out of alignment. Since most of the Cambodians would never need to touch a blade to their faces in their entire lives, they probably were marveling at this American ritual of early morning self-mutilation, undoubtedly meant to invoke true warrior spirit. Fortunately, I had a styptic pencil to help seal off the bleeding, and I was able to finish the shave, ever so carefully.

Later that morning, I presented my scarred visage to Col. Hoang Tich Thong, the commanding officer of Brigade A. Even by diminutive Vietnamese standards, Colonel Thong was the runt of the litter, short and scrawny with buck teeth that gave him a vaguely rodent-like appearance. Back in Saigon, I had heard a lot about him. The senior Vietnamese Marine officers were rather a clubby lot, and Thong definitely was odd man out. Not interested in popularity, he remained one of the six most powerful and respected Marine officers because he was highly professional. But he was not in a position to make any mistakes, because he did not have any friends who would forgive them. Thong seemed to realize this and reveled in living on the edge. The more he felt threatened, the better he met the challenge.

As I was ushered into Thong's command post, an attractive young Vietnamese woman slipped out a back door, with a furtive glance in my direction. She was wearing a gray uniform similar to that of a Red Cross "doughnut dolly"—but I didn't see any doughnuts in the room. Colonel Thong's greeting was proper enough, but he showed little of the major's cordiality the evening before. I guessed that the stories about him were true and began to hunker down inside. But Thong was basically in a good mood as he talked of the recent assault into Prey Veng, a provincial capital just north of Neak Luong. In a six-day fight, the South Vietnamese Marines had killed 295 North Vietnamese, while losing only seven of their own. He took me out to the porch and showed me a Chinese-built antiaircraft gun, one of seven crew-served weapons they had captured. I had heard a lot about this from the major and from earlier briefings; it was the first time the VNMC had conducted combat operations without their co-vans, who were forbidden by a presidential executive order to go any deeper than twenty-five miles into Cambodia. Neak Luong was as far as any of us could go.

But the brigade had another operation coming up that would take it back toward the Vietnamese border, so the co-vans were back in the game. The target was at least a part of the elusive Central Office of South

In June 1970, Col. Hoang Thich Thong, commanding officer of Brigade "A" (later redesignated Brigade 147), poses with a Chinese-made antiaircraft gun captured from the North Vietnamese Army during fighting at the Cambodian provincial capital of Prey Veng.

Vietnam (COSVN) headquarters, which supposedly controlled all the Communist political and military efforts in the South. The location and composition of this command-and-control agency had been variously reported in Vietnam, in Cambodia, and on the border. COSVN fragments were said to consist of anything from tiny, highly mobile command cells to an underground headquarters, located in a maze of tunnels and compartments. At any rate, our objective was a thickly wooded area, right on the border. We would conduct a one-battalion heliborne assault, with reinforcements standing by to be lifted in as necessary. If we got lucky, we could strike a severe blow to enemy operations in the South, further expediting the withdrawal of U.S. troops and placing the South Vietnamese in firmer control of their own destiny. If not a war-ender, it could be a big step in that direction.

As Colonel Thong continued to talk, it became increasingly clear that he would not be seeking my tactical advice in planning this operation. He could plan stuff like this in his sleep. After all, he had been fighting *somebody* ever since the creation of the Vietnamese Marine Corps back in 1954. He had been a brigade commander for several years; I had less than one year of combat at rifle company and infantry battalion level, although—frankly—his brigade-level setup didn't look as complicated as our old First Battalion, First Marines combat command post, and his battalion commanders seemed to run their units largely out of their hip pockets, the way our company commanders did.

The biggest difference between the U.S. and Vietnamese command set-ups lay in their means for coordinating and controlling aviation and indirect fire support—and that's where the co-vans came in. My job on this upcoming operation would be to work with the U.S. Army aviation unit that provided both helicopter troop transport and gunship support.

My confidence soared after the first planning session with the Army folks. They were a self-assured, almost cocky lot, who acted as though they had done this hundreds of times—and some of them probably had. They wore black cowboy hats, supremely indifferent to the connotation of "black hats" in general and of "cowboy" from the Vietnamese perspective in particular. In terms of exotic headgear for U.S. forces, on the other hand, I recognized that my own French-made green beret had to be some-where near the top of the list.

Despite their bigger-than-life initial impression, these Army gents were deadly serious professionals when it came to the business of flying in harm's way. In addition to their highly maneuverable transport helicop-ters, they flew heavily armed gunships and light observation helicopters—the LOH, or "Loach." To say that the Loach was solely an observation air-craft would be a major understatement. Often, its mission was to draw fire from the ground by jinking and buzzing and popping up so close to the earth that after a while very few gunners could resist the temptation to take a potshot. Accordingly, the Loach was actually designed to crash. In a worst-case situation, its bubble-shaped cockpit would break off and roll away from the long, skinny fuselage and tail rotor, which could crumple and sometimes burn. Much more often, however, the gunner would miss; the Loach would dance away, reporting the gun's position to the armed helicopters orbiting high overhead—and the gunships would roll in hot, firing machine guns and rockets at the gunner who had just made the final mistake of his suddenly truncated life.

Such hair-raising tactics required a special breed of pilot, illustrating a difference between naval (Navy and Marine) aviators and the daring young men who flew the Army birds. The naval aviators were college grad-uates in their mid-to-late twenties; all of them had gone through basic flight training at Pensacola, then advanced training in their rotary-wing specialty before receiving their wings of gold. Their ears were highly attuned to the sounds of potential malfunction, and they didn't push the envelope when it came to matters of maintenance, crew rest, and other considerations of flight safety. This was partly because many of them were married, with children and mortgages and large life-insurance policies.

Most of the Army pilots, on the other hand, were nineteen-year-old warrant officers who, like most other nineteen-year-olds the world around, believed they would live forever and didn't give a rat's ass for the moon. If the troops on the ground didn't break faith by bringing them into hot landing zones without warning or committing other such stupidities, they gladly would push any envelopes to bring them the aerial support they needed. To these fearless fliers, a gut-wrenching roller-coaster ride in a Loach through enemy ground fire was all in a day's work.

The final planning did not take long. The Sixth Vietnamese Marine Battalion, commanded by Maj. Do Tung, would be the assault force. The Sixth Battalion's senior advisor was Maj. Gene Adams, a West Pointer. This was looking more and more like an Army show, but so be it. We would be launching at first light.

By the time we had loaded, launched, and assembled the first waves and approached the objective area, the early morning overcast had burned off and the sun was shining through. This part of the border was not solid jungle but one of several heavily wooded areas with distinct edges, separated by green fields. If anyone tried to escape, we would spot him from the air sooner or later. We had two command-and-control (C&C or "Charlie-Charlie") birds in the air. One carried the Army aviation commander, who deftly controlled the transport and close air support helicopters while bringing in the first waves; the other carried Colonel Thong, talking to Major Tung on the ground, and me, talking to Gene Adams.

Because the Army's heavy-lift helicopter squadron could not carry the entire Sixth Battalion in one lift, a two-stage operation had been planned. Half the battalion and Major Tung's command group would land first, set up a temporary defense against counterattack, then go on the attack when the second wave arrived after a forty-to-forty-five-minute turnaround.

This arrangement carried some built-in danger. If we had indeed found part of COSVN or another senior enemy headquarters complex, it certainly would be heavily defended from the outset, so hitting pay dirt also meant landing in the middle of a hornets' nest. On the other hand, failure to ignite an immediate response was no guarantee that the enemy would not launch a strong counterattack. No matter how we cut it, most of that first hour on the ground was going to be tense—for all of us.

The turnaround and troop pickup stayed on schedule, and as soon as the transport helicopters came into view again I radioed Gene Adams to "pop a smoke"—that is, to mark his landing zone with a smoke grenade. Early in the war we had learned not to announce the color when popping a smoke, because the enemy listening in would then pop the same-color smoke in a half-dozen locations, hoping to lure an unwary helicopter pilot into a trap. I would have to tell Gene what color smoke I saw, so that he could confirm that it actually was his. The only trouble was that the trees were so tall and the canopy was so thick that I could see no smoke at all as we circled overhead.

"Gene—I can't pick up your smoke. Did you pop it yet?"

"Affirmative," came the reply.

We waited another agonizing minute or so. Then it was Gene's turn, with tension rising in his voice:

"See it yet?"

"No joy. Still looking hard."

"Well, look harder. It's got to be up there by now."

After another small eternity, a wisp of green smoke escaped the tree-tops.

"Okay—I've got your green. . . ."

"*Yes!* It's *green!* It is definitely *green!*"

I know how Gene must have felt, because I felt the same sense of relief.

As the operation wore on, it became increasingly apparent that the intelligence estimates of the COSVN headquarters location had been wrong. This time out, it would not be a replay of Prey Veng. We would not be poking a stick into a hornets' nest—or even a gnats' nest.

After more fruitless searching on the ground, we saw a half-dozen cyclists emerge from the woods, pedaling toward the nearest village. Not long afterward, a new American voice broke into my advisor radio net. The intruder was a rear admiral, the senior U.S. naval officer in the Mekong Delta and the second-ranking naval officer in country. Normally, generals and admirals get to break into just about any radio net they choose, because they usually are in charge of all the nets in their area. But this was a Vietnamese show, and this admiral was not in the Vietnamese chain of command. (For that matter, *I* was not in the Vietnamese chain of command; we were advisors in fact as well as in name.) I have no doubt that this admiral—hereafter identified as The Admiral—was fully aware of this arrangement as his own personal helicopter lifted off the flight deck of his flagship, the USS *Benewah* (a converted riverine barracks ship with the graceful lines of a Sears, Roebuck warehouse, anchored in the Mekong River). But by the time he reached the objective area, circling—godlike—high above the action below, he undoubtedly had convinced himself that he was not in the *chain* of command—he was *in* command! Therefore, when he saw those bicyclists pedaling down the road, he was duty-bound to stop them. He told his radio operator to enter the English-language net he had been monitoring, my advisor net.

"The Admiral says stop those bike riders," the radioman said.

"What!?"

"Stop the bikers, they're getting away."

"Roger. Wait. Out."

This was ridiculous. The nondescript bike riders, carrying virtually nothing with them, evidently had pedaled through the wooded area en route to the next town. The Sixth Battalion was searching a distant part of the woods, supported by the Loaches and gunships. The transport helicopters had gone home to refuel. The only way Colonel Thong could stop the bikers was to land his own Charlie-Charlie bird directly in front of them, relinquishing control of his operation for some indefinite period, even while things still were somewhat intense. But I had to relay the message.

"The Admiral wants us to stop those bike riders."

Colonel Thong responded with an impatient toss of his head, which seemed to say, You handle it. I've got a war to fight.

Back on the radio, I tried to be diplomatic. "The brigade commander's respects to The Admiral, and he has given his suggestion the highest consideration—but because of the tactical situation he is unable to comply at this time. Over."

"Wait, over."

The reply was not long in coming. "The Admiral directs your counterpart to report to his flagship at 1300 today. Out."

Unbelievable! And they weren't even going to wait for a response. Talk about hit and run. . . . I tried to dead-pan it, as I relayed the message to Thong. "He wants you to report to his flagship at 1300."

Thong just smiled. It was kind of a wolfish smile—or as wolfish as somebody with buck teeth could bring off. I got the message. Report to The Admiral at 1300? No way.

Then we turned back to the business at hand. But somehow, I sensed that we probably had not heard the last from The Admiral.

Within another hour, it became evident that we would not find anything significant on this particular day. As the Sixth Battalion completed its sweep through the wooded area—finding virtually no evidence of bunkers, fortifications, or even recent encampments—we called for the transport helicopters to begin picking up the troops and then turned back toward Neak Luong. Beneath us, the bicyclists were still pedaling gamely toward the first village inside Cambodia. Colonel Thong caught my eye, gestured toward the pilot of our helicopter, and pointed downward. I switched on the intercom to talk to the pilot.

"Take us down, and land close enough in front of those bike riders to stop them. Don't shut down."

"Roger. Going down."

As we touched down, Colonel Thong motioned for me to stay in the bird and jumped out without even loosening the flap on his holster. Sure enough, the bike riders were fully as innocuous as they had looked from the air. To my novice eye, they looked Cambodian—the westernmost province of South Vietnam in this area had essentially an ethnic Cambodian population, governed by the Vietnamese—but even if the riders were Vietnamese, they were obviously not North Vietnamese or Vietcong leaders in disguise. And unless they could magically break down their bikes and turn them into AK-47 automatic rifles, they were unarmed. Thong talked easily with them for a few moments, then waved them through and got back on the bird. Thus ended the Great Bicycle Threat.

Back at Neak Luong, we picked up the rest of the story. The Admiral, on the *Benewah* when the cyclists were first reported, evidently had assumed that they were part of the COSVN staff, fleeing from the Vietnamese Marines. The *Benewah* had a three-inch naval gun mounted on her bow, and The Admiral ordered its crew to fire on the cyclists. The gun chief explained that the gun was not mounted on a stabilized platform and therefore would rise, fall, and tilt in accordance with the wave action of the river flowing by. In addition, there was no linkage with a naval gunfire spotter ashore, so the crew would be unable to adjust fire onto the target. Undeterred, The Admiral decided to become an airborne spotter and immediately took off in his own helicopter.

Once he had the cyclists in sight, he called for a spotting round. The gun fired, but The Admiral could see no sign of impact. He called for another round, but the result was the same. After a half-dozen futile tries, the gun chief explained that he had no white-phosphorus spotting rounds, which left highly visible puffs of white smoke upon impact. He didn't even have high-explosive rounds, which left visible dirty black smoke and were appropriate for soft ground targets. In fact, all he had was armor-piercing ammunition, which left few traces of its point of impact.

At this point, the thoroughly frustrated Admiral broke into the advisor net. His mood could hardly have improved after receiving the wave-off from Colonel Thong and must have hit bottom when he returned to the *Benewah* and was handed a message from the Commander, Naval Forces Vietnam, the only in-country naval officer who was senior to him. Evidently, someone on his staff had dutifully reported up the line the uninvited, uncoordinated, and uncleared naval gunfire into the VNMC area of operations. The message was terse:

POSITION AS COMMANDER OF NAVAL FORCES IN THE DELTA DOES NOT INCLUDE DUTIES AS NAVAL GUNFIRE SPOTTER. CEASE AND DESIST.

Back at Neak Luong, as well, another war was under way.

The river crossing site was a natural wayside stop for travelers en route to Phnom Penh. Most of these seemed to be journalists or visiting Congressional delegations, code-named CODELs, like some type of cough syrup. And the brand of syrup they were peddling was hard to swallow. The party line being sold back in the States then was that the so-called invasion of Cambodia was just the latest display of animosity between two populations that went back hundreds of years and that, with American encouragement and support, the South Vietnamese were raping, pillaging, and generally making life miserable for the innocent people of a neutral country. This, of course, was utter baloney, but after the Silly Sixties, many Americans were ready to believe anything, especially about two small countries they couldn't even locate on a map. Over the years, the mood of the American people had shifted from "win and get out," to "win or get out," to "get out."

In reality, of course, we were not fighting Cambodians. We were fighting against units of the North Vietnamese Army, which had occupied the border region and points inland for years. They had been there so long that North Vietnamese troops were breeding with Cambodian women to produce a mixed race of Viet-Cambot children.

We had, in fact, released a number of political prisoners of Cambodia's Prince Sihanouk, who had attempted to stay in power by acquiescing to North Vietnamese demands while posing as a fiercely independent sovereign. After these men showed us extremely moving poetry about freedom and liberty, written while in confinement, they went out to organize self-defense battalions to fight the hated North Vietnamese—the *real* invaders. They drilled without weapons, hoping to acquire some from the South Vietnamese.

On one of these CODEL visits, a congressman managed to unearth some truth he had not been seeking. He told me that he wanted to see evidence of all this raping and pillaging. I replied that he would have one hell of a time finding any around Neak Luong, which was the only part of Cambodia we'd seen close up. Undeterred, he said he wanted to walk into town and take a look for himself.

A true zealot is one who, upon finding that his efforts have taken him off course, redoubles his efforts.

Accompanied by a U.S. Marine gunnery sergeant who was a Khmer-language interpreter, we started down the dusty road toward town. Before long, we encountered a Cambodian civilian headed our way. He was decked out in a South Vietnamese field uniform, complete with jungle boots. Although he wore a cartridge belt, he had no weapon of any sort and lacked headgear. Most likely, he was from one of the self-defense battalions, drilling every afternoon while hoping to be equipped by the South Vietnamese to take the fight to the communists.

"Where did you get your uniform?" asked the gunnery sergeant.

"I bought it from a Vietnamese."

"Where did you get your boots and cartridge belt?"

"I bought them from a Vietnamese."

"Where is your weapon?"

"I don't have one—but I hope to buy one from a Vietnamese."

Shaken but undeterred, the congressman continued his march into town. As we approached the first buildings, a Vietnamese Marine and a Cambodian civilian—an unlikely duo, by any reckoning—swung into view. Evidently, the two of them had spent a long afternoon at the town's only sidewalk café. They moved toward us in true drunken-sailor fashion: leaning inboard, with arms around shoulders, and singing lustily like long-lost buddies.

That did it. The congressman turned on his heel and walked directly back to his waiting helicopter. I don't know what he told his colleagues and his constituents after he got back to the States; somehow, I doubt it was the truth.

The journalists we encountered, on the other hand, had moved beyond the initial rape-and-pillage story line. Aware of the executive order that called for all U.S. military personnel to be pulled out of Cambodia by 30 June 1970, they were beginning to push the line that horrible disasters would befall any South Vietnamese units remaining in Cambodia after the Americans left. This was errant nonsense, of course—the Vietnamese Marines' smashing success at Prey Veng, without direct advisor support, proved otherwise. But this line pandered to the misguided emotional outbursts back in the States, culminating at Kent State, over the "fact" that we now were in the business of invading neutral countries.

Once again, reality lay elsewhere. The U.S.-Vietnamese incursion into Cambodia had dried up long-held Communist border sanctuaries and severed the waterborne supply route through the Cambodian port of Sihanoukville. This was designed to let us disengage U.S. forces from the Mekong Delta under minimal military pressure, and did so. President Richard Nixon had been elected in 1968 with a mandate to extract our nation from the quagmire that the Vietnam War had become. Less than two years later, the withdrawal was in full swing and accelerating daily.

What tragic irony that Nixon—even with his Watergate-shortened second term—was destined to preside over more wartime days than Woodrow Wilson and Franklin Delano Roosevelt combined.

On one sunny Sunday afternoon, I ran into a journalistic one-two punch.

First into the picture was Morley Safer. I knew something about Safer, a Canadian journalist employed by CBS News. I doubted his credibility right off the bat because I had heard his televised report on the torching of Cam Ne village back in 1965, which was allegedly staged. (I also had heard that television executives interviewed by a USMC captain subsequently admitted that they were trying to destroy Lyndon Johnson, whom they considered an unworthy heir to the Kennedy throne. And what better way to bring down a sitting president, than through selective reporting of an unpopular war?)

So I watched Safer warily as he approached our brigade command post that afternoon. He was stopping by on his way to Phnom Penh, to see how the Vietnamese Marines were doing. He glanced at our situation map. Not much was happening that day, but I mentioned some recent successes. He switched on his tape recorder.

"Yes, but how will they do after all you advisors have to go back into Vietnam?"

"They'll do fine. They won big at Prey Veng without our direct assistance, when we couldn't go north of here. And look at the buildup of supplies and gear going on right here. They are preparing for the long haul."

This probably was not what Safer wanted to hear, but he was cordial as he turned off his recorder, thanked me, and moved on.

Minutes later, a young reporter for one of the wire services came through. He also looked at the situation map; he had a question about one of the tactical symbols. "That's the Second NVA Division," I explained. "After our big fight there," I continued, pointing on the map, "they had pulled back to lick their wounds, but our units are still making occasional contact with elements of that division in the general area." The North Vietnamese were not showing much stomach for another big fight just yet.

I did not know how well things were going outside of the VNMC sector, but I told the reporter that we were doing okay and the VNMC would continue to do okay after the co-vans had to head back to South Vietnam at the end of the month.

The next day, I heard a fragment of a disturbing story on an Armed Forces Radio newscast—something about the Second NVA Division being poised to strike the provincial capital of Prey Veng shortly after the advisors pulled out, or some such crap. Wondering briefly where that came from, I turned back to business. But later that afternoon, Lt. Col. Pat McMillan, Assistant Senior Marine Advisor, flew in from Saigon for an unscheduled visit, bearing copies of that morning's newspapers. Evidently, the wire service bureau chief had cobbled together stories from several reporters scattered throughout Vietnam and Cambodia, running the summary under his own byline. It being a rather slow news day, he had only one quotable source: a Major John Miller, advising Marine Brigade A in Cambodia. Thus: "'The South Vietnamese forces are spread thinly over four fronts,' said Major Miller. . . . 'The Second NVA Division is poised to strike Prey Veng,' said Major Miller. . . . 'The South Vietnamese effort in Cambodia will collapse after 30 June, when the advisors leave,' said Major Miller" by now the leading pundit and prognosticator of the war.

"He should not say these things!" screamed Lt. Gen. Le Nguyen Khang, the commandant of the South Vietnamese Marine Corps, in Saigon.

"Well, maybe he didn't—you know how reporters are," said Col. William Van Zuyen, the senior Marine advisor. So he dispatched Lieutenant Colonel McMillan to find out.

When I saw the newspapers, I was outraged. I wanted to hunt down that miserable reporter and bureau chief and rip their faces off. But McMillan advised prudence. "We know the real story now. This will be forgotten in a few days. If you stir things up, they will start to stink again."

In fact, things did settle down quickly, after two minor aftershocks. A few days later, I received a tear sheet from the international edition of the *New York Herald-Tribune* from a worried former college roommate, then living in London. There it was—my Cambodian quote-a-thon splashed on page one above the fold, as the lead story of the day. Bad news travels fast and far.

A week or so after that, I received a cheery letter from my wife back in Norfolk, with a small tape recording she had obtained from a friend of ours, a broadcasting professional. She had been rinsing the lunch dishes and just about dropped a plate when my voice cut through loud and clear on our kitchen radio—during a piece by Morley Safer on the CBS noontime news, anchored by Douglas Edwards in New York. After Safer had popped the question about how the Vietnamese Marines would do after the advisors left, my politically incorrect reply came through unaltered and undistorted. But such an against-the-grain comment could not be allowed to stand as the last word on the subject. Edwards deftly stood me on my head before he moved on to the next story:

"Of course, the major is entitled to his own opinion, but *we* all know that the embattled Vietnamese face. . . ."

Even if the reporters were telling it straight, the editors had the final word in perpetuating the party line.

But my wife didn't care. She was just happy to have this confirmation that I was warm and breathing at the moment. The last time she had received news related to me over the radio, it had been a 1965 report that "a company of the First Battalion, First Marines" had been overrun, with nine fatalities and about fifty wounded. I commanded D Company, First Battalion, First Marines at the time, and she was in government quarters at Camp Pendleton, California.

Hearing the news, my wife bundled up our two-year-old daughter and drove to Palomar Mountain for the day. If the official sedan with the chaplain and the casualty assistance officer drove up to our quarters, she would not be there—and thus my death would not have occurred. Then we'd all start over and maybe things would work out better next time. This approach may have been a bit existential, but we all cope in our own ways.

The official dispatch actually had read, "A [as in Alpha] Company. . . ," so she needn't have worried about me at all. Instead of scaring the daylights out of the families and friends of two hundred Marines in Alpha Company, the clueless announcer had scared the loved ones of more than a thousand Marines—an entire battalion.

As Lieutenant Colonel McMillan had predicted, the dust eventually settled, with no permanent damage. Nevertheless, I could not escape the nagging reality: Inside of two weeks in Cambodia, I had managed to get myself on the hit list of the senior admiral in the Mekong Delta, the U.S. media, and the Commandant of the Vietnamese Marine Corps. In retrospect, I was in danger of violating Hartmann's Law of the Conservation of Enemies: Friends come and go, but enemies accumulate, and one must take care not to accumulate any more enemies than can be handled at any given time.

At least my fellow co-vans still believed in me. And the best was yet to come.

Chapter 3

As things turned out, the Second NVA Division did not wait for the co-vans to leave before going on the attack again. A few days after the unfortunate wire-service article, elements of that division launched a night assault against the Second Marine Battalion in the Prey Veng area, on the heels of a hundred-round mortar barrage. The NVA paid dearly, pulling back at dawn after losing more than forty men killed in action, as opposed to six VNMC dead. They continued to pay for the next two days, as the VNMC moved the Sixth and Seventh Battalions into blocking positions, forming an anvil of sorts, and the Second Battalion counterattacked, becoming the hammer that pounded the retreating NVA mercilessly, killing another seventy of them—at a cost of fifteen more Marines killed—until whatever was left of the battered NVA force managed to break contact.

The VNMC wounded—and later the dead—were lifted out of Neak Luong by helicopter. In the aid station where the wounded were stabilized for travel, the mood was generally somber, but with an undercurrent of jubilation, except for the most severely wounded. They had kicked ass again, and now they were going home for a while. After the surgeons had worked for most of an hour removing mortar or grenade fragments that had peppered his legs, one young Marine began to come out of anesthesia, slowly. Before he was fully awake, he put one hand under his blanket and reached for his groin, to check out the family jewels. Evidently, they still were intact because he withdrew his hand, sighed deeply, and went back to sleep with a smile on his face. He never had opened his eyes.

Considering that these Vietnamese men were in for the duration, unlike the Americans and their one-year tours, such lightness of spirit in the midst of chaos and suffering was an unexpected yet welcome part of their makeup, lying just under a fatalistic attitude toward combat that sometimes caused them to accept risks that were unnecessary. What the hell—if the only ways out of this unhealthy situation were in chains or feet first, why worry about a few risks here or there?

Such sudden mood shifts were nowhere more apparent than at the helicopter landing pad, where medics and stretcher bearers waited with their wounded buddies for the evacuation birds. The mood was somber, out of respect for the injured. But after the final stretcher had been loaded and the final helicopter had lifted off, the healthy Marines almost instantaneously fell into a laughing-and-scratching mood, joking about—for example—the unfortunate Marine who had been wounded in the hindparts and had to be evacuated face down on his stretcher.

After a while, maintaining a sense of humor is the only way to maintain your sanity.

The wounded were evacuated quickly, but soon it became apparent that transporting the dead would be a problem. Other combat missions had priority; the dead could wait, despite the effect their lingering presence had on the living. After two more days, most of the twenty-one bodies had been taken off, but six still remained, lined up in their body bags beside the helo pad. Angry clouds of flies buzzed about the supposedly airtight bags. From time to time, Marines with bandanas over their noses and mouths would spray something on the body bags, but within an hour or so, as soon as the new dark green wet slickness had baked dry in the intense heat, the flies would be back. Imperfectly contained, the smell of death began to spread through the area, no matter which way the wind was blowing.

With no medevac helicopters in sight, the idea arose to take the bodies by small boat down the Mekong to the Vietnamese border for further transportation to Saigon. But there were several practical difficulties attached to this, not the least of which was finding a willing crew for the small boat. Finally, Colonel Thong had seen and heard enough. He got on the radio and evidently managed—over the airways—to strike terror into the heart of one or more appropriate functionaries, because within two hours a medevac helicopter landed, loaded the bodies, and took off.

Not long afterward, a body floated down the Mekong and lodged in some underbrush on our bank. The corpse was face down and severely bloated, and had been in the water long enough for a great deal of pigment to be washed out of its skin. It was a sickly white with faint yellow undertones, so it probably was Asian, of indeterminate nationality. It appeared to be hairless. Its arms were bound behind its back, and a jagged piece of board protruded from one side, where it had been driven through the rib cage. It was hard to tell where this apparition had originated, but as a working party struggled to free the body from the underbrush and take it away for disposal, several possibilities emerged. Maybe it was a Cambodian village official, who had run afoul of the North Vietnamese—or for that matter, a North Vietnamese soldier captured by vengeful Cambodian villagers, although his civilian working trousers that looked like pajama bottoms seemed to belie that. Or it might even have been the loser of a Cambodian-on-Cambodian fight deeper in the hinterland. Some of those enthusiastic young warriors had been photographed marching around with their enemies' heads stuck on spears, so a board through the ribs would be no big deal.

Whatever had happened, this was clear evidence that there was a lot more war going on in this country—farther up the Mekong, deeper into the heart of darkness—than the war we saw immediately before us. And if anything, it was even more savage than ours, if that piece of board protruding obscenely from the rib cage was any indication. And it would continue long after we Americans went back to Vietnam at the end of the month, and even after the VNMC returned, possibly months later. So what difference did we actually make? And if it was not all that much, what in bloody hell were we doing there?

After that three-day flare up, things settled down for a while. As the 30 June deadline for all Americans to leave Cambodia neared, I heard from Lieutenant Colonel McMillan again, by radio:

Our interesting compatriot, The Admiral, had decided to pull out all the

co-vans from Brigades A and B to take them to South Vietnam on his flagship. Aside from the fact that he had not talked to our seniors about it,
his plan would make the *Benewah* an especially tempting target for NVA
fire from both banks of the Mekong. MacMillan did not want so many
of his advisory eggs riding in that lone basket; instead, he wanted us back
in Saigon and Thu Duc. The training center and dependents' quarters
needed a lot of work, and we needed co-vans on the scene to supervise. In
addition, the senior U.S. Army advisor in the Rung Sat, a colonel named
David Hackworth, also was working his bolt, trying to get advisors coming
out of Cambodia assigned to him. The Senior Marine Advisor in Saigon
had fought off that request for the time being, but all the co-vans needed
to be gainfully employed to make his efforts stick.

"So set up a helicopter—quietly—and get them out of there before The
Admiral captures them for his boat ride. And don't forget Bill Healy."

Capt. Bill Healy, the junior advisor to one of the infantry battalions,
was already a prisoner of The Admiral, who had shanghaied Bill several
weeks earlier to be his daily ground combat briefer, an underwhelming
assignment for someone who was supposed to be *in* combat, not briefing
it. I had talked with Bill on an earlier visit to the *Benewah,* and he was truly
one unhappy soul.

I gave a heads-up to Maj. Ted Bierman, the senior advisor to Brigade B,
and asked him to alert Bill Healy. Then, with just a few days to go, I flew
back to Chau Doc, a South Vietnamese border town, to line up the transport helicopter. Chau Doc was a fair-sized town, with a large military
compound run by the U.S. Army that supported all services of South Vietnam and the United States. In one sense, it was the Southern California of
Vietnam, a final collection point for folks who, for whatever reasons, had
moved westward through Vietnam until they could go no farther. In
another parallel to Southern California, Chau Doc and its collection of
independent spirits provided a breeding ground for a number of distinctive
religious sects—such as the Hoa Hao and the Cao Dai—which believed in
everything from animism to Victor Hugo as a patron saint. On my first
morning there, at breakfast in the spacious base mess hall, an Army officer
was regaling me about the peculiarities of the town and the region when
he stopped in mid-sentence:

"See what I mean? *Look!*" he said, pointing at the Vietnamese waitress who was picking up our dishes.

She had six fingers on her left hand.

The Chau Doc base had a sizable air strip and was geared to handle a lot of transients, so the evening before I had no trouble finding a comfortable metal bunk in a strong-backed tent, with a wooden deck, a screen door, and screening on the open sides—breezy and bug-free. After dinner at the mess hall—especially fine, after several weeks of C-rations—I was able to watch a fairly recent movie in an open-air theater before turning in. I didn't even miss my own personal bat zooming across the co-vans' back porch.

Comparatively speaking, this was Hog Heaven, and I couldn't really fault any transient who might wish to extend his stay here. The permanent base personnel didn't seem to be particularly overworked, either. At this late stage of U.S. involvement, they seemed to be engaged mainly in taking in each others' laundry, amid generally benign surroundings. Their latest military scare had come during the Tet Offensive more than two years earlier, and they hadn't been threatened since. In fact, with the ongoing operation in Cambodia, the communist forces' presence in the entire region had dried up, leaving everyone feeling safer than ever. Chau Doc could almost qualify as a rest and recreation center.

Maybe that was a good thing, because there were a lot of burnouts walking around on that base. The next morning after breakfast, I returned to my transient quarters briefly before getting on with the business of the day. One officer was still in his bunk and showed no signs of moving. I asked if he was feeling sick. No, not at all, said the officer, who later identified himself as a U.S. Army major. It was just that this was his *fourth* tour in Vietnam; we hadn't won yet; and we were packing up, getting ready to go home without winning. So why should he get up before noon? The longer he slept, the faster the time went until he got to go home again.

And this guy was drawing the same amount of pay from the grateful taxpaying citizens of the United States that I was.

A land-line call to the Army's heavy-lift helicopter squadron at Can Tho—the "Innkeepers"—laid on the bird for 28 June, and I was able to get back to Ted Bierman to confirm the arrangements: The Great Escape was on! I stayed in Chau Doc to ensure that the escapees would make a trouble-free reentry. There was no point in going back for just a day or so, with no operations pending—and this was not a bad place to wait for things to happen.

The day of the Great Escape finally arrived. The Army CH-47 Chinook arrived at Neak Luong on time, and Ted Bierman had all the advisors ready to load on board with all their gear.

The loading was nearly complete when The Admiral, having flown in from the *Benewah* in his own personal helicopter, landed nearby. He could not believe his eyes. The Chinook was fully loaded, and the rear ramp was beginning to go up.

"Where do you think you are going?" he screamed at Ted, another West Pointer who had found his way into the co-vans. Standing in the aftermost part of the big helicopter, Ted drew himself to full cadet rigidity and held a perfect hand salute while intoning—as the rising ramp blocked more and more of his body from view, Cheshire Cat style—"Sir, I have my orders from the Senior Marine Advisor."

The ramp snapped shut and the pilot put on power for takeoff, leaving The Admiral in a swirling mixture of dust and debris. He was beside himself. He immediately flew back to the *Benewah,* leaving his own personal helicopter turning and burning on the flight deck while he went down to the radio room to fire off a "what-the-hell?" message to Saigon. In his haste, rage, and confusion, The Admiral had failed to notice his ground combat briefer, co-van Bill Healy, sitting quietly on the flight deck with all his gear, as instructed. The timing of Bill's Freedom Flight was still uncertain, but Bill filled in the blanks by throwing his gear into the back of The Admiral's helicopter and telling the pilot to take him to Chau Doc. Evidently figuring that The Admiral had cleared this short hop—after all, who would have the balls to commandeer The Admiral's own personal helicopter?—the pilot lifted off without delay.

The Great Escape was complete.

That evening, the liberated co-vans gathered in the rather large quarters of the Senior Province Advisor for an impromptu celebration. Things were just beginning to get a little drunk inside when the telephone rang. It was Lieutenant Colonel McMillan:

"John—great job in getting the advisors back, but The Admiral is in orbit. He had wanted to muster all U.S. naval personnel on the fantail of the *Benewah,* to be sure that everyone got out on time. But I told him that the Senior Marine Advisor didn't receive his order for that, and therefore could not comply."

McMillan added that Healy's imaginative escape had pushed The Admiral over the edge, so I'd have to send Bill back until things cooled down. He probably wouldn't be back there for long. With all the advisors out of Cambodia, Bill had no firsthand sources of information any more. So The Admiral would eventually let him go—after he had saved some face.

Red Rover—Red Rover. Let Bill Healy come over. . . .

The next morning, I sent Bill back to the *Benewah* and launched the rest of the co-vans on a motor march back to Saigon. Then, for a couple of days, I poked around for ways to support the Marine brigades in Cambodia from the Vietnamese side of the border.

I went over to the local hospital to see if any VNMC casualties lingered there, but all the wounded Marines had been taken to Saigon. I was impressed by the cleanliness and good order of the hospital but was saddened to see so many beds in passageways and balcony walkways, because the wards were so full.

The air facility at Chau Doc was a non-starter, as well. No U.S. aircraft could fly into Cambodia any more, and distances were short enough that Vietnamese aircraft could operate from their own fields. Next, I went out to the headquarters of the nearest ARVN division, which might have offered a way to monitor the tactical situation in Cambodia and even communicate with the Vietnamese Marines in the field under special circumstances. But this ARVN division was strictly a territorial outfit; it was not about to leave its comfortable stomping grounds for Cambodia or anywhere else. The tip-off should have come when I saw two of their armored personnel carriers on the road, with dainty parasols shielding their drivers from the sun, in addition to the hog wallow in the middle of the division command post. For anyone who might have thought that the division commander had the slightest interest in monitoring the situation in Cambodia, it clearly was a case of mistaken identity. After these false starts, I finally concluded that we could do a better job of helping our field commanders from the Bo Tu Lenh in Saigon, with long-haul communications and access to the Vietnamese Joint General Staff. Chau Doc's value as a way station had evaporated along with the American presence in Cambodia.

By then, it was the Fourth of July—and there was another party at the quarters of the province advisor, a rather large civilian gent whose preferred working and social uniform was a set of jungle utilities dyed black. This time, I was the only co-van in a house filled with a variety of civilian and military types.

The party grew and grew, and grew louder and louder as more and more people drifted in and adult beverages continued to flow. In time, I found myself locked in heated debate with a cynical civilian from AIDS or COORDS or another one of those alphabet agencies designed to win the hearts and minds of the Vietnamese people. Seeing that there was nowhere for this discussion to go but physical, an Army captain intervened and said quietly to me, "Let's get out of here, and show these assholes a real Fourth of July!" And so we did.

As things turned out, the Army captain was part of one of those shady programs designed to eliminate the Vietcong infrastructure, a "shadow government" of sorts itself, through assassination and other means that were generally objectionable to nice people—the same nice people who were too ill-informed to realize that the Vietcong had been employing the same techniques for years. He lived in a safe house in the middle of town, guarded by Chinese mercenaries. We drove through the deserted streets to the house, passing through the sentries—big, mean-looking brutes—and climbed three flights of stairs to the roof.

The flat roof was ringed with a short wall of sandbags, with which the captain could shield himself from small-arms fire while awaiting emergency liftoff by helicopter. In one corner was a 60-mm mortar and a plentiful supply of signal flares for use in emergencies. Tonight was the time to commemorate the Glorious Fourth and offer the entire world, starting right here, its chance to rejoice in the shining reality of American independence.

And thus we became mortarmen, filling the night skies over Chau Doc with a fireworks display not seen since the Tet Offensive of 1968. The reaction in town was marvelous—first, the lights going on; next, the sirens revving up from various locations; and finally, the screeching sound of official vehicles of various types burning rubber as they sped to uncertain destinations. Woke them up, we did. Three cheers for the Red, White, and Blue!

The next day, I went back to Saigon, in a jeep—something I could not have done a few months earlier. The Cambodian incursion had indeed dried up the Delta.

But up north, the war was still on.

Chapter 4

Once I was back in Saigon, it did not take long for a new assignment to materialize. Brigade B, now comprised of the Second, Fifth, and Sixth Battalions, was being pulled from Cambodia, redesignated Brigade 256, and moved up to the northernmost Military Region I (I ["Eye"] Corps, in U.S. parlance) in Quang Nam Province, for Operation Vu Ninh XII. At the same time, Gene Adams, senior advisor to the Sixth Battalion, decided to extend his tour by six months (what the hell—he was single) and thus became eligible for six weeks of R & R (rest and whatever) in Australia. Soon after Gene had helped settle the Sixth Battalion into Vu Ninh XII, some twenty-four kilometers southwest of the U.S. Marine combat base at An Hoa, I would relieve him. The target area was Vietcong/NVA Base Area 112—a complex trail network, often covered by double and triple canopy jungle, over which the Bad Guys operated their most active logistics support operations in South Vietnam. Base Area 112 also was a natural marshaling area for rocket and ground attacks against Da Nang and the heavily populated lowlands of Quang Nam Province. So Vu Ninh XII offered a real opportunity to disrupt the enemy's operations and seize his caches of arms, ammunition, and other vital supplies. It all sounded great on paper—just like our attack on the supposed COSVN headquarters in Cambodia.

Getting to Vu Ninh XII was going to be half the fun. It would be a three-stage trip.

The first stage led to the First Marine Division headquarters complex at Da Nang, where I bunked in with some old friends on the division staff. The whole division, not just those who had completed a full year's tour, was packing up and getting ready to go home, as part of the highly accelerated withdrawal from Vietnam, begun more than a year earlier in the name of "Vietnamizing" the war. Reconnaissance units were doing most of the heavy lifting by then, sending small "Stingray" teams deep into enemy territory—clandestinely, when possible—to call in devastating air and artillery strikes. Whenever these teams were discovered by searching communist forces, we had to extract them by helicopter, a difficult and dangerous operation. Later that year, supervising one such extraction would cost the life of the Recon Battalion commander, Lt. Col. Bill Leftwich, who had received the Navy Cross for heroism during a prior tour as a co-van and was so revered as a combat leader that he was being touted, even at this mid-level stage of his career, as a future commandant of the Marine Corps.

But there was no hint of that future tragedy, still a few months distant, as I gathered with some division staff officers on a wooden patio to burn some steaks on an outdoor grill and sample some well-made martinis (one was just right; two were too many; and three were not enough), watching the sun go down past the forbidding mountains and valleys to the west. I recalled patrols and operations in Happy Valley, Elephant Valley, and Antenna Valley from my time in this area five years earlier. And I remembered that beneath the lush canopy in that beautiful rugged terrain lurked the ever-present heat, mud, treacherous footing, leeches, and entangling vines that had to be overcome en route to meet the enemy. Within hours, I would be back in those forbidding hills—well beyond them, actually. But that time would come quickly enough. Vietnam could be a beautiful, exotic place at sunset, with the war suspended for a few hours. Why not seize the moment?

It was an extraordinary evening. I could feel a strong current of cynicism under the surface festivities. "Disgruntled staff officer" had always been a redundancy, to my mind, but some of these guys were long past disgruntled—deeply bitter, and viciously witty about it. As more of the officers reached the "not enough" stage of martini consumption, the many and varied stories of the many and varied inadequacies of the political and military hierarchy—national down to local—got funnier and funnier. These were not sour draftees, yanked kicking and screaming from their jobs and schools into hazardous military service at coolie wages. These were long-service professionals, bringing years of training and experience to bear in what once had seemed to be the national interest, only to see a failure of leadership, beginning at the very top. It was a hilarious but profoundly disturbing evening.

The next morning, I caught a helicopter out to An Hoa, where the Fifth Marine Regiment occupied a combat base that looked almost like a medieval fortress. The layers of sandbags around the bunkers had been painted with a black sealant of some sort, giving a first impression from the air that the place had been constructed of boulders. The proud fighting history of the Fifth Marines stretches back to Belleau Wood in World War I, and this day's bearers of the regimental colors were dug in so deeply against occasional small-arms and mortar attacks that they looked as though they were back in the trenches at Verdun.

Once on the ground, I saw quickly that the initial impression of military preparedness had been an illusion. Nobody expects a combat base to resemble a parade ground, but in terms of actions and appearance these were the sloppiest U.S. Marines I'd ever seen. I didn't see any luggage lying around, but it was evident that these troops had already packed their seabags mentally and were just waiting around for the order to get all their stuff in one bag and get on the truck to go home. I felt doubly let down, because my first assignment a dozen years earlier had been as a rifle platoon leader in the First Battalion, Fifth Marines, and we had taken strong pride in looking and acting like professionals, even in the field—especially on the field of battle.

Maj. Gene Harrison, who had relieved Ted Bierman as the senior advisor of Brigade 256, met me at the An Hoa helicopter strip and drove us out the Fifth Marines' gate—manned by an unshaven, shirtless Marine wearing an unzipped flak jacket and a graffiti-filled helmet cover—to the nearby VNMC brigade command post. Gene's setup was more austere and less fortified, even though it was actually exercising command and control over three infantry battalions in the field, sweeping through Base Area 112 toward the Laotian border.

Gene and I had served together in Norfolk two tours earlier, then had attended the three-month Marine Advisor Course at Quantico just before coming over. There were fourteen officers—captains and majors—in our class. The course goals were straightforward. We were there to freshen our fire-support skills, with hands-on training in spotting rounds on Quantico's artillery ranges, at the naval gunfire trainer on the amphibious base at Little Creek, Virginia, and in the back seat of a T-28 aircraft, which I had first ridden as a midshipman fifteen years earlier (and which today stands mounted like a museum piece on a pedestal in front of the officers' club at the Naval Air Station, Corpus Christi, Texas). We also practiced air-ground communications from the ground. We contacted aircraft literally out of the blue and talked them over to where we were standing in a very small clearing in a very large woodland, which we would have to do in calling for close air support for VNMC units on the ground. As events had already proved, this was extremely valuable training—far more extensive than the average infantry officer ever gets.

Nevertheless, most of our time was spent in total-immersion Vietnamese language instruction. Unlike the language training offered at Fort Bragg to U.S. Army advisors, among others, our training focused on grammar and structure as we built vocabulary, so we could truly learn the language if we put enough time and effort into it. The Fort Bragg course, on the other hand, provided long lists of handy phrases for rote memorization, with little or no idea of the underlying language structure. But Fort Bragg had one thing that Quantico didn't have, and that was Vietnamese instructors. Our instructors were U.S. Marines who had served with interrogator-translator teams, grilling prisoners of war. They were fluent enough and probably had learned from native speakers themselves, but our learning from them was roughly equivalent to making a photocopy from a photocopy. We were two steps away from the original, and not quite as precise with our tones.

As a tonal language, Vietnamese can assign multiple meanings to the same word, depending on the way it's said. For example, *"ba,"* spoken with a flat tone, is the number three. But *"bạ,"* with a low, guttural grunt, means a married woman. (It's not hard to see why old Mrs. Nguyen might get bent out of shape if referred to as "Number Three Nguyen.") The net result of our total-immersion training was an uncertain mastery of a third language—a tongue alien to both Vietnamese and English speakers but perfectly clear to us co-vans. Once we got to Vietnam and were totally immersed in native speakers, most of us made the necessary adjustments.

Instead of rattling off handy phrases, we memorized dialogues from a small handbook: "Ow! I'm hit!"—"Are you hurt bad?"—"Naw, it's nothing—just a broken arm."

This sent us on a frantic but fruitless search through the glossary for terms that might be more useful (if not critical) for us—such as "sucking chest wound," or "gunshot wound, head," or "multiple fragmentation wounds, lower extremities."

We decided to chide our instructors for the handbook's shortcomings by creating our own tongue-in-cheek dialogues: "I am an American Marine officer"—"I have a low threshold of pain"—"What do you wish to know?" That set the instructors to thumbing frantically through the book: "Where does it say *that?*"

Gene Harrison's assistant brigade advisor was Capt. Butch Neal, in his final two or three months of a tour that already had seen him receive two Silver Star medals for heroism in the Mekong Delta. After Gene had read me into the situation and Butch had provided a few tips on lightening the load in my pack, it was time to go back to the Fifth Marines' area to wait for my Vietnamese Air Force helicopter ride out to the Sixth Battalion.

On the way back, I told the young Vietnamese driver to let me out of the jeep well before we reached the Fifth Marines' perimeter. I didn't want him to become disillusioned by seeing a raggedy-ass sentry like the one I had seen on the way out. The Vietnamese Marines took so much pride in patterning themselves on their U.S. counterparts that the shock would have been severe.

Carrying my pack and all the gear I would be taking to the field, I hiked through the gate and headed for the helicopter strip. About halfway through the area, I heard a terrific racket coming from what appeared to be a sandbagged slop chute. I set my gear down and took a look inside. There—in the middle of the day . . . in the middle of the week—a young female go-go-dancer was gyrating around on a stage, leading a packed house of sweaty young Marines in song. The place was hotter than hell; even if the air conditioning was up and running, it would have been overwhelmed by sheer animal heat. Even the go-go song leader, tastefully dressed in next to nothing by the USO or whomever, was glistening as she belted out such classics of the day as "I've Got A Ticket To Ride," and "I've Got To Get Outta This Place."

The warriors. The tip of the spear.

Fortunately, I did not have long to wait at the helicopter strip before my ride showed up. It was a Vietnamese Air Force Huey helicopter, carrying the VNMC paymaster on his appointed rounds to fire support bases and battalions in the field. We took off and flew westward toward the Laotian border, past an area known as "Arizona Territory" to U.S. Marines who had fought there. The helicopter pilot flew as though he were being pursued by all the imps of Hell, skimming along at treetop level, barely clearing steep hills, and plunging into valleys. The final plunge was the steepest, and it felt as though we were going all the way in; I could not be certain that we would even have a controlled crash. But the pilot eased his descent and we settled to the ground like a feather.

Gene Adams was waiting in the small clearing where we settled down, with an appropriately big smile and the obligatory small packet of maps, which there wouldn't be time to explain because the paymaster had to complete his rounds before sunset. After the pilot took Gene back to An Hoa, he had to return here immediately for the paymaster.

Déjà vu all over again.

As the helicopter lifted off, a young Vietnamese Marine stepped into the clearing and motioned with his head for us to follow him. He took us to a narrow trail, which soon began to climb up a steep hillside through dense undergrowth. I was bigger to begin with, and the only one carrying a full pack, so I had to do some brute-force trail-breaking, while the other two slipped through the openings in the brush easily. It took about fifteen strenuous minutes to reach the top of the hill, where I stood, sweating and red-faced, before Maj. Do Tung, commanding the Sixth Battalion. Tung was cool, in every sense of the word. A true aristocrat, he spoke excellent English:

"You may wish to freshen up. Your cowboy will help you get squared away. We will have dinner in forty-five minutes."

I looked around the small battalion command post, which seemed to blend into the jungle. A few low tables made from small tree branches lashed together were used for eating and map work. Jungle hammocks, with tops and mosquito netting on the sides, were strung on trees adjacent to the relatively few cleared areas. As a rule, nobody slept on the ground except for those manning the defense perimeter, unless we were in direct contact with the enemy. A number of small cooking fires dotted the area, and the battalion's staff officers and Marines talked quietly in singsong voices as they moved about. Everything seemed self-contained and

This Vietnamese "cowboy"—nicknamed *Gà Chết* (literally "dead chicken," as in chicken-run-around-with-head-cut-off)—took Saigon to the field in the form of his transistor radio.

purposeful, in such contrast to the sweaty, raucous self-pity I had recently left behind.

I had arrived at the eye of the storm: a Shangri-La, a new world—where all that mattered was the here and now and the task at hand. All other distractions had been lifted away and I could feel, physically, a great weight being lifted from my shoulders, even though I still was wearing my pack. I was home, half a world distant from all that had been familiar in my life up to now, but right in the middle of everything that mattered for the time being. I did not understand much about this new world yet, but I felt that I was on the edge of something profound, which was waiting to be discovered when the time was right.

With the help of my cowboy, I was ready by dinnertime, with gear unpacked and hammock strung. Calm and cool, I responded to the cowboy's dinner call: *"An cơm, Thiếu-tá"* ("Eat-rice, Major"). And rice it was. One small bowl of it, with a couple of shreds of meat on top, seasoned by as much *nước mắm* as anyone might dare use. I did not use very much. After dinner, there was a piece of fruit for dessert. Major Tung's mother, who lived in Da Nang, brought a basket of fruit to the Da Nang airfield every fourth day, when our resupply helicopters loaded up. The Sixth Battalion was therefore known as a good feeder—for Major Tung and his senior staff officers, at any rate. Six or eight of us dined together, and it was nice to be included, even though there was not much conversation.

There was one other meal each day, in the late morning, which usually consisted of a bowl of rice without the meat and fruit. As a concession to the American breakfast tradition, however, most cowboys would make a cup of chickory-flavored Vietnamese coffee for their co-vans shortly after first light, pouring off the excess hot water into a cup of dried Chinese noodles. This was a great way to jump-start the day, especially if we were going to hit the trail early, and those noodles were every bit as tasty as the ones you could get from a street vendor in Saigon. At the time, I tried to recall one interpretation of Chinese history as a series of epic struggles between the rice-eaters from the South and the noodle-eaters from the North. It seemed that the noodle-eaters usually prevailed, but either way the co-vans had that bet covered.

Two small bowls of rice, a cup of noodles, a bit of protein, and a piece of

Maj. Do Huu Tung *(right)*, commanding officer of the Sixth Battalion, confers with two staff officers and co-van Capt. Pete Anderson in his field command post west of An Hoa, during Operation Vu Ninh XII.

fruit was adequate daily fare for a ninety-eight-pound Vietnamese, but for a co-van at something close to twice that weight, it was a sure-fire recipe for weight reduction. Most co-vans experienced a quick ten- to twenty-pound drop once they reached the field. Some actually shrank. One battalion advisor, Capt. John Admire, scaled down to such an extent—remaining in perfect proportion all the while—that he became known as the Incredible Shrinking Co-van.

Most of the Americans took this in stride, chalking it up to the price of doing business in this aspect of the war. But on rare occasions, an advisor who had spent most of his (arguably) adult life bulking up for beauty would watch in shock, horror, and finally full panic as his abs, lats, and pecs continued to shrivel visibly, day by day. If he gave way to his fears and began trying to hog food in the field and plead for dietary supplements to be sent out on the resupply helicopters, he had begun to cook his own unsavory goose. Such an attitude would only disgust the Vietnamese, and his credibility as an advisor would plummet with such a loss of face. Before long, he would be pulled from the field and sent home, with a less-than-glowing fitness report about his incomplete combat tour marring an otherwise fine service record.

Of course, nothing kept the Vietnamese Marines from augmenting their field rations with a bit of rod-and-gun work, when time and circumstances permitted. Late one afternoon, the Sixth Battalion uncovered an abandoned North Vietnamese Army base area, and Major Tung decided to stop there for the night. While the command post—hammocks, little tables, and all—sprang up around us, we studied the tactical map and made plans for the next day. As we began, the sound of a single rifle shot reverberated through the jungle. *Some klutz has cranked off a round accidentally,* I thought. I glanced at Tung, looking for signs of annoyance. Accidental discharges, in the field or in garrison, have been known to drive U.S. commanders to raging peaks of temporary insanity. But Tung continued to study the map, unperturbed. Evidently, he had decided to play it cool. Fine; then I wouldn't bring it up.

Minutes later, I heard a faint rustling sound directly behind me. I turned slowly, then nearly leaped out of my skin as I found myself snout-to-snout with a wild boar, tusks and all. Much too slowly, my field of vision widened and I could see that the boar's head had been severed from its powerful body. It was held aloft by the grinning young Vietnamese Marine who had downed the boar with a single shot.

My recoil action could not have been more violent if I had stepped on a rattlesnake. "Nice shot," I said, trying to regain composure. But I hadn't fooled Tung and his staff officers. To their credit, they didn't laugh openly—but they smiled a lot, in a sly way. Maybe I had passed some kind of a test, after all. At any rate, there would be extra pork on the table for the next few days.

For me, the transition to the rice-and-roots diet was not difficult. After a day or two, I found myself hungry at mealtimes but satisfied afterward. And in the jungle heat, lighter is better because it puts less strain on one's system. I still had occasional fantasies about my first big steak dinner back in civilization, without fully realizing how difficult that ultimately would become. I supposed that I was shrinking like the other co-vans, but without bathroom scales or even a mirror, it was hard to keep track.

Much later, back in Saigon, the cumulative change became clear when another advisor attempted to encircle my right bicep with his thumb and forefinger and almost made it (well, he had big hands). "Had polio lately?" he asked casually.

I wasn't as gaunt as Ted Gatchel (thank God), but I was getting there.

At the time, however, I was less concerned about wasting away and more concerned about passing my first test in combat with the Sixth Battalion, to win full acceptance as a co-van. Anyone who would actively wish to get into a heavy firefight is clearly a moron, but that was just about the price of admission to this elite club. It was our own Catch-22.

Some co-vans gained entrance to the club by solving knotty tactical problems for their buddies. One of the earlier advisors in the Delta grew frustrated by a series of harassing twilight 82-mm mortar attacks on his battalion's command post. Deciding to take things into his own hands, he began with a quick analysis: The Vietcong would fire a couple of rounds and be gone before the Marines could return fire. That meant that they must have set up their mortar at nearly the maximum range of the VNMC's 81-mm mortars. Since overland movement in that swampy terrain was nearly impossible, the gunners must have traveled by boat. With his command post location at the center, the co-van drew a maximum-range circle, representing 3,750 meters, on his tactical map. He looked at places where the circle intersected waterways, then looked for nearby clearings large enough to set up a mortar. One location fit.

Next, he registered one of his mortars on that clearing, traveling upstream for a visual check for accuracy. He sandbagged the mortar in its firing position and staged a few rounds nearby. As dusk approached, he sat beside his mortar, with a round in hand. As soon as he picked up the first incoming round, he dropped his round down the tube and ducked, then dropped another round. A quick boat trip to the clearing revealed one destroyed mortar and two dead gunners.

Life for that co-van began to improve immediately.

Chapter 5

My first firefight with the Sixth Battalion was not long in coming.

Late one afternoon, we found a river-crossing site near the Laotian border that showed signs of use by the North Vietnamese. Going by recent activity in the area, we figured that they might try to use it again soon. Major Tung directed one of his rifle companies to set an ambush along the NVA's most likely route of approach to the crossing site. Then the rest of the battalion began the climb into the high ground overlooking the river valley. The battalion command group set up shop just below the crest of a prominent ridge line, about one thousand meters from the ambush site, which still was in view. The jungle hammocks went up quickly—a good thing, because it began to rain early that evening.

Around midnight, all hell broke loose. Our ambush company had caught a North Vietnamese sapper company, on its way south to blow up a few things we wanted to keep intact, dead in its sights, halfway across the river. As the small-arms firing built up, I heard the droning of a propeller-driven aircraft approaching us. I couldn't see anything in the rainy darkness, but the bird sounded as though it could be a "Spooky." A Spooky was a large transport aircraft rigged with Gatling guns that could fire upwards of seven hundred rounds per minute in an angry roaring buzz, with devastating effect on the ground. Used against troops in the open, it could cut huge swaths of total destruction, virtually vaporizing everything in its path. Still in my hammock (why run around in the rain?), I tuned my radio to the Spooky frequency and tried to make contact. On the first call, the answer came back, loud and clear. Spooky was ready to play.

Major Tung, still in *his* hammock, was talking to his ambush company commander, setting up a system for aerial fire support. The company commander had a flashing strobe light that could be seen from the air, despite all the rain and gloom. He radioed to Major Tung the range and bearing from his flashing light to the target. Then Tung called the target information over to me, in the quiet, matter-of-fact voice of a poker player asking the dealer for more cards. Emulating Tung's calm demeanor, I sent the range-and-bearing instructions up to Spooky. After Spooky's first pass, the company commander provided corrections to adjust the fire onto the target—moving it up or down, and right or left—and we repeated the process.

Spooky stayed on station for thirty to forty-five minutes, as best I can recall. Time speeds by when it is evident that you are winning on the battlefield; it drags much more slowly when you are not sure whether you are winning or losing (especially when you suspect that you are losing), until it's all over. By the time Spooky left our area, however, the rout was complete, as the remnants of the North Vietnamese force broke contact and tried to melt away in the dark—back north, to lick their wounds. Weeks later, back in Saigon, I was able to hear a radio-intercept tape of the NVA commander relaying his plight to senior headquarters. Perhaps unaware of Spooky's role in ripping up his sapper company, he estimated that he was surrounded by a full infantry battalion—a force three or four times the size of the company he had actually encountered.

The next morning, the VNMC ambush company commander recovered a lot of enemy weapons. This was highly unusual, because the NVA had formidable battlefield discipline and seldom left behind valuable gear of any sort. In this case, their highest priority must have been retrieval of their wounded and dead; there were signs in the jungle that many bodies had been dragged away under cover of darkness.

By early afternoon on the following day, the ambush company commander and his troops had joined the rest of the battalion in the hills. With a huge grin, he personally presented an armload of captured weapons to Major Tung.

Then the Sixth Battalion had a party.

Actually, the party had been in the works for some time—but in this case the timing was impeccable. What better time to toast dangers shared and victories won? Two resupply runs earlier, Tung had asked me to arrange for the beer through U.S. channels. There was a hierarchy of beers to be observed. Schlitz beer was for the officers; Miller beer was for the noncommissioned officers and troops. This did not mean that most officers preferred Schlitz and most of the other ranks preferred Miller; it meant that *all* officers drank Schlitz and all others drank Miller. And nobody drank Pabst Blue Ribbon, because that was Air Force beer.

But the truly unique thing about these parties in the field was the food. Accustomed to two bowls of rice per day, we suddenly were engulfed in everything *but* rice—small cubes of meat and other delicacies wrapped in leaves, exotic fruits, and the like. And there was a ton of this food. The thing to do was eat until you ached; it was just like my first evening in Cambodia. How a bunch of people accustomed to living on two bowls of rice a day could wrap themselves around so much party food remains a mystery to me. Maybe they had digestive systems like those of snakes and could walk around for days with swollen bellies, digesting away until everything they had ingested was all gone.

As a matter of fact, I had noticed the same thing with regard to a young Vietcong *chiêu hồi* defector on my first Vietnam tour five years earlier. After he came over to our side, one of his first acts was to wolf down about a week's worth of C-rations, which are designed to provide about four thousand calories per day to large, growing Americans engaged in the equivalent of hard labor. At first, he almost looked pregnant, and he didn't eat very much during the next few days on the trail. But he never showed discomfort during the intake or discharge phases.

But back to the party. It was easy to join in the party spirit as the Marines celebrated their great victory, and I quickly fell into the mutual back-slapping. I felt quite at home. After all, I had played a part in that victory. I also had arranged for the Schlitz and Miller beer.

Parties in the field were hardly commonplace, even for the VNMC. But a party on the last night before the start of a new operation was a way of life for them. After all, who knew how many of them still would be standing at the end of the operation? This points up a difference between U.S. and Vietnamese battle philosophies: Most of the U.S. combat commanders knew they had only one year to make their mark. Some had only six months, under a hideously shortsighted policy of maximizing command ticket-punches at the expense of the troops. They tended, as a result, to be impatient. As quickly as they could arrange it, they would go clattering into battle with a great show of ferocious energy.

But a few weeks later, especially during the winter monsoon, they would be ready to come back out, with more and more troops suffering from immersion foot and other wetness-related ailments, and more and more gear becoming soaked and inoperative. Even worse, although the extreme fatigue imposed by the weather and terrain would barely match the stress of being shot at by a determined adversary, it was a strong contributor to a breakdown in the will to fight.

The Vietnamese, on the other hand, would make their preparations and move toward the sound of the guns in an entirely different manner. On the eve of battle, they would have their party, celebrating among themselves despite odds of survival that were decreasing steadily as they moved closer to the battleground. Then, the next morning, having said their good-byes to those still unknown who would not be returning, they would sling their weapons and field gear and move back into combat, prepared for the long haul.

Because they generally knew the weather and the terrain—although the men from the South had some real problems adjusting to conditions in the Middle Region and northward—they knew how to get these elements to work in their favor, rather than complicating their lives or even destroying them. Just by stringing hammocks, for example, they generally slept high and dry, unbothered by whatever crept or slithered along the ground at night. A sudden tropical downpour always was welcome. It cooled the air, sent fresh rainwater cascading down the roofs of the hammocks into waiting containers, and even provided Mother Nature's freshwater shower baths to the Vietnamese, dancing around in the rain with bars of soap in hand.

Faced with a similar downpour, U.S. ground-pounders would be sitting in deepening mud, wondering when their ponchos would stop keeping them dry, as inevitably they would. Even when the semi-waterproof pon-chos kept the rain out, it got so hot and steamy inside that the wearer soon would be soaking wet. So why not take off the miserable thing and get soaking wet in a cooling rain? On balance, the Vietnamese put a more practical spin on the semi-cynical adage, "A good foot soldier stays warm and dry at all times"; it generally applied unless it was time for a shower.

Nevertheless, as Operation Vu Ninh XII went past the one-month mark, the Marine brigade was beginning to take casualties beyond those the enemy was inflicting. Accustomed to operating in the Mekong Delta, the rice bowl of the entire region, also laced with waterways that teemed with seafood, the Vietnamese expected to eat well. But in Quang Nam Province, in the Middle Region, the rivers and streams were better suited for crossing than for fishing. When the brigade began to ship troops back to the rear with symptoms of malaria—chills, fever, the whole nine yards—or possibly the dreaded break-bone fever, the U.S. Navy's preventive-medicine specialists took an urgent interest in the problem.

As they looked at mosquitoes or other possible disease vectors without success, however, a miracle seemed to occur: The hospitalized troops were recovering far more quickly and completely than the blood-fever cases, so chasing mosquitoes was following a false trail. Looking for pollutants in the waterways also proved fruitless. Even after the men were ordered to use halizone tablets to purify the water in their canteens, the "malaria" cases continued to arise. Then the medics zeroed in on a change that occurred after the Marines were hospitalized: Their diet suddenly became more sub-stantial, especially with regard to protein intake, and recovery began immediately. With protein deficiency finally identified as the culprit, the medics could take action. They couldn't do much about the basic food sup-ply in the Middle Region, but they could start sending food supplements out with the resupply helicopters. And the Vietnamese who had sneered at those few panic-stricken advisors who had called for supplements in the field could swallow a little pride along with their own pills, to make the problem go away—which it did, in time.

This episode reminded me of an earlier co-van preventive-medicine program. Several years earlier, one advisor carried a rainy-day precaution—a fifth of Johnny Walker Scotch whiskey—in his pack. One day, it really came in handy. His battalion had a chance meeting with another VNMC battalion on the trail. As many of them loved to do, the two battalion commanders quickly fell into a game of "my co-van can beat your co-van." After a while, the claims and counterclaims had escalated to the point where the Scotch-bearing advisor's counterpart could pull out a small vial of bat's blood and announce grandly: "My co-van can drink bat's blood!"

Wondering where his buddy had obtained that miserable vial of blood, the advisor felt his self-preservation instincts kick in and decided to ratchet up the bidding one more notch. Reaching into his pack, he announced—equally grandly: "I do not stop at drinking bat's blood—I drink bat's blood and *Scotch!*" Then he poured that horrible mixture into his canteen cup. And as he drank it down as fast as he dared, he only could hope that the Johnny Walker was potent enough to kill off the parasites that were bound to be in the bat's blood before they got into his bloodstream.

It worked. The co-van saved face, for his buddy and his own sweet self. The other battalion commander certainly lost face. And parasites never showed up to haunt the resourceful advisor.

As a rule, each VNMC battalion had two advisors, a major and a captain. But in jungle-search operations like Vu Ninh XII, they usually split up to cover more ground. The co-van major would stay with the battalion commander and the Alpha group; the captain would go with the executive officer and the Bravo group. The only times I saw Capt. Pete Anderson, the other Sixth Battalion co-van, were during our occasional meetings on the trail. The rest of the time, as much as I tried to turn Vietnamese, I couldn't quite get there.

Part of the problem was language. My Quantico brand of Vietnamese was adequate for shooting the breeze with the troops, once I got on top of my tones. We could talk about where our homes were, how many brothers and sisters, and the like. The effort was generally appreciated. Most of the officers were fluent in French, but I wasn't. I was fluent enough in Spanish for real Spaniards to recoil from my horrible Andalusian accent, but this avenue of communication was a non-starter for the Vietnamese. So I talked with the officers mostly in English. Several of them had at least one year in an all-English setting at Marine Corps Schools, Quantico, after some formal English schooling in Vietnam. I had my three-months' total immersion with the interrogator-translators. We could deal with military terms with appropriate precision and take the level of conversation up another notch or two higher than my all-Vietnamese chats with the troops, but we seldom found ourselves pondering the Fate of Nations over our evening bowls of rice.

It is a truism that a soldier is never alone, and that is nowhere more true than with an infantry unit in the field. Yet at the same time, it is possible to feel lonely even when surrounded by friends, especially if you are not communicating on all channels. Occasional glimpses of U.S. helicopter crews, under helmets and behind windshields on resupply runs every fourth day, were some reassurance that I had not lost my own identity. I made another, more profound form of contact with the West one Sunday morning when things were quiet. I switched on my transistor to Armed Forces Radio, which usually featured an endless stream of air-headed disk-jockey material, broken by occasional news briefs. That morning, however, I caught the front end of a half-hour broadcast from Salt Lake City of music and the spoken word, featuring the Mormon Tabernacle Choir. The following Sunday, I was able to tune in at the same time and struck pay dirt again. From then on, even back in Saigon, I kept that radio date whenever I could. It was a much-needed anchor for my soul.

Not all my radio contact with the West was quite so sublime, however. My brief experience in the Delta had taught me why the co-vans had a mutual love affair going with a U.S. Army heavy-lift helicopter squadron, the "Innkeepers." On the ground and in the air, we would take extra risks for each other, and we both could count on it. West of An Hoa, however, we were being supported by a Marine Corps heavy-lift squadron, the "Dimmers," and our radio encounters were not nearly so cordial. Instead of brothers-in-arms, they seemed to regard the Vietnamese ground units almost as supplicants, barely deserving of any support, even though they were carrying the brunt of the fighting while U.S. units packed up to go home. Forget about them going the extra mile; they sounded reluctant to go the required mile. And sometimes they would get downright insulting.

Often, a co-van would have to leave his radio propped against a tree with his squawk box turned up high while he went about other business in the command post. When an obnoxious American voice came booming through with something like, "How many slopeheads (or zipperheads, or gooks) are we going to lift today?" it could make things sticky, even when the co-van showed immediate displeasure and gave the bird a return blast. Most of the Vietnamese in that command post understood enough English to know when they were being insulted.

Of course, the co-vans had the ability to talk among themselves on the advisor radio net, but they generally had the self-discipline to keep the net clear for tactical traffic. Sometimes around sunset, however, if things were otherwise quiet, three or four co-vans would meet on the net for a bit of quiet, reassuring chatter before dark. The infantry advisors on the ground would be feeling relatively secure, down in the weeds; the artillery advisors on the fire support bases were perhaps enjoying a few more creature comforts, but also were feeling a good deal more exposed.

The VNMC had established two firebases on high terrain at the outset of Operation Vu Ninh XII, then added two more a couple of weeks later. It did not take these stationary targets on prominent terrain features very long to attract the attention of enemy mortar and rocket gunners—especially on resupply days, when the added presence of slow-moving helicopters made them doubly attractive. One of these bases fell under the purview of Capt. Bob "Magnet Ass" Wills, an experienced cannon-cocker who had the unfortunate habit of acquiring shell fragments in his *gluteus maximus*—but not enough yet to be sent home under the three-Purple-Hearts-and-out rule (as though Bob ever would have to tried to go out that way).

On one sunny morning, Magnet Ass was trying to run a resupply operation for his firebase but was getting a lot of grief from enemy rocket gunners every time a helicopter approached with much-needed supplies. Because flying conditions were ideal, however, he was able to build a formidable stack of fast-burner U.S. Navy, Air Force, and Marine attack aircraft—orbiting at nicely separated ascending altitudes over the firebase. He would bring the jet aircraft in hot, two at a time, to destroy the enemy rocket sites, or at least to neutralize them while the gunners tried to clear the ringing from their ears. Then he would bring in the helicopters, hovering and moving slowly across the landing pad—almost touching down but not quite, as the crews pushed supplies over the lowered rear ramp—then flaring off quickly into an ascent once the delivery was complete. By the time the enemy gunners were able to man their weapons again, that phase of the resupply was over. Then Magnet Ass would bring in two more fast-burners and begin the process all over again.

Down in the weeds with the Sixth Battalion, I was monitoring this spectacular Magnet Ass Aerial Circus on my tactical radio, marveling at such a great show staged on our behalf. After a while, I could hear the distinctive putt-putting of a Huey command-and-control helicopter, headed toward the firebase.

The next sound on the net was the voice of Magnet Ass, in considerable pain and anguish.

"Get outa my stack!"

After identifying himself, the aircraft commander announced that he was inbound to the firebase, with a Code Six on board. A Code Six meant that it was probably a general or an admiral, or some equally high civilian. It was time to clear the decks for landing and prepare to conduct arrival honors. But Magnet Ass had a different take on the situation:

"I don't care if you have Our Lord and Savior on board! Get outa my stack or I'll shoot you down."

There was no response. For the next few minutes the only sound was of the helicopter reversing course, with the familiar putt-putts growing fainter as the aircraft moved toward the horizon.

We waited for retaliation to come thundering down our convoluted chain of command. But it never did. Either the Code Six who got the wave-off from Magnet Ass was unable to find us, or he experienced a sudden attack of common sense somewhere along the line.

After running for five weeks or so, Operation Vu Ninh XII ground to a halt, not long after the one-day aerial circus. The official word did not come down until close to the final day, but the troops around Major Tung's command post seemed to know quite a bit earlier, probably because of radio traffic overheard and passed on to their friends by the enlisted radiomen. Communicators are always the first to get the Word.

My first inkling came one morning when I heard a cowboy singing "Saigon . . . Saigon" (*Shy-gun . . . Shy-gun*) softly to himself as he lit a small cooking fire. For all but a few permanent residents of the Middle Region, Saigon was as distant as Paris—a city they would never see. To them, the notion of Saigon being the seat of government, as Washington, D.C., is seen by most Americans, was so hazy that it did not exist. In the Middle Region and throughout the Vietnamese countryside, the seat of government—and the central fact of life—was the village.

For these Vietnamese Marines, most of them recruited from the South, going to Saigon meant going back home, or close to it. This was not a problem-free experience for everyone. Some came from villages in the Mekong Delta where the Vietcong had exerted control at night for years. And some of them, in a post-boot-camp burst of bravado, had had the words *Sat Cong* (Kill Vietcong) tattooed on the backs of their hands, near the web between thumb and forefinger. When they returned home, nobody faulted those young warriors for having second thoughts about their own survivability and carving away those two words that might have gotten them disemboweled some dark night. But as the Delta continued to dry up in the aftermath of the Cambodian incursion, the number of hands with the tell-tale tattoo-removal scars continued to diminish.

For the Sixth Battalion, Operation Vu Ninh XII ended abruptly with a helicopter lift back to the An Hoa combat base, by now almost deserted. The U.S. Fifth Marines were long gone, and a small contingent of logistical support types was overseeing the removal of supplies and equipment that still remained on the base. Their thin and lax security setup was mute evidence of their guesstimate that the likelihood of attack was small—even though a German-run orphanage in the area had been overrun and burned just days earlier. The surly American cargo-handlers—just as clueless as the previous occupants of this miserable collection of painted sandbags—seemed concerned that their Vietnamese brothers-in-arms, returning from the battlefield, might try to steal something. But they had little to fear. Without incident, the real warriors moved through the deserted combat base and into assembly areas for rest and restaging for the return trip to Saigon.

Three of us—the three senior battalion advisors from the Second, Fifth, and Sixth Battalions—stayed behind at the An Hoa helicopter pad. We had some unfinished business with the First Marine Aircraft Wing, back in Da Nang. In particular, we had a bone to pick with the Dimmers. We found the heavy-lift squadron on a Sunday morning and presented ourselves— three overheated and underdeodorized USMC majors in tiger suits and green berets—to the adjutant. We identified ourselves by our radio call signs. Mine was "Grizzly Grips Sierra."

"Oh, Lordy—," was all the adjutant could say, as he scrambled from behind his desk in a high-priority search for the squadron's executive officer.

Chapter 6

It did not take long to find the executive officer, and when he appeared I could not contain my amazement. He was Maj. John Carroll, every inch a gentleman, in the finest tradition of his aristocratic Maryland namesake. The year before, John and I had been classmates at the Armed Forces Staff College in Norfolk, and members of the same eighteen-man seminar group. Because the class consisted of field-grade officers from all the armed services, plus civilian officials from the departments of defense and state, plus a sampling of allied officers, the first weeks of the six-month resident course had to be devoted to service orientation, for greater mutual understanding. The students made the presentations to their seminar mates. Our seminar was the only one with two Marines, so John and I decided to give a double-barreled pitch—the full Marine Corps air-ground team treatment. And in the first drowsy hour of that fateful Monday morning, as our seminar mates cast wary glances at the boom box in the back of the room, steeling themselves for such mood music as the Marines' Hymn, John and I started in—explaining that this indeed was a glorious day in their hitherto incomplete lives. They would be learning about the inner workings and hidden mechanisms of the Corps that they "might someday be fighting alongside, and trying to keep up with. . . ." With that, we switched on the music, but it was not the Hymn. It was the "Hallelujah Chorus," from Handel's *Messiah,* sung by the Mormon

Tabernacle Choir in full throat and backed by the full power and majesty of
Eugene Ormandy and the Philadelphia Orchestra, with the volume turned
all the way up to ten. It was truly a moment of revelation for our startled
classmates.

So John and I were kindred spirits. And he was generous to a fault and a
good listener to boot. Everything was going to be all right. John followed
attentively as I moved to the heart of the problem. When I had finished, he
said, "The problem is that we need to get educated. Only three of our
pilots—the commanding officer, the operations officer, and I—have been
in-country before. And they are pushing these young guys through flight
training so quickly these days that they don't even get a shot at Basic
School."

I had forgotten. A few years back, in an attempt to keep the pilot seats
filled in Southeast Asia, the Marine Corps had abandoned its longtime
practice of sending all newly commissioned officers—air and ground—to
The Basic School at Quantico, where everyone learned the rudiments of
being a rifle platoon commander, the better to support riflemen on the
ground in later years. All these new guys knew was the stick and something about their birds—and not much about why they were flying.

"So educate me," John said. "Tell me what we need to know about the
Vietnamese Marines and how you operate—and I'll sure educate these
young pilots. They are ready to learn; we just haven't told them enough of
the right things."

Operation Vu Ninh XII had ended, and we were about to leave the area,
so whatever educating there was going to be would have to be done that
day. John invited us to begin the process with a steak-and-eggs squadron
brunch, just getting under way. By the time we had finished holding
school, it was late afternoon and the squadron was firing up the grills for a
steak fry. Clearly, the First Marine Aircraft Wing was not on the verge of
developing any protein-deficiency problems.

After the extended rice-and-roots diet in the field, broken only by that
post-ambush party, the moderate portion of steak and eggs served at
brunch had been a nice change of pace. But the he-man steaks at the afternoon fry were something else. Reality did not set in right away, but before
long my system went into full rebellion, and I was sick as a dog. In a sud-

den flash of insight, it became clear to me why most Vietnamese will turn green when confronted by a big slab of meat.

By then, it was too late to catch a helicopter back to the VNMC positions at An Hoa, so we looked for a place to bunk in. The nearby III Marine Amphibious Force headquarters had a transient facility, but it had been filled for the evening by advisors and various support types coming in from Vu Ninh XII. We set out for China Beach, also in the area. If we had to sleep under the stars, at least the sounds of the surf and sea birds would be a pleasant change from the sounds of the jungle at night. But before long we stumbled across a bunker, right on the beach. It had real beds—not folding cots—made up with sheets, blankets, and pillows. There was a small desk inside, as well—not quite the Holiday Inn, but not too shabby, either. A safe haven if the command building came under rocket or mortar attack, it must have belonged to one or more of the generals. Since we were already well into a quiet evening, we gambled on the general or generals not needing it that night. And if they did, we would certainly get out of their way. Rank hath its privileges. I fought back the temptation to slip between the clean sheets; that might have been pushing our host's hospitality a bit much. I flopped on top of the regulation-tucked blanket and slipped instantly into the dreamless sleep of the pure in heart.

The sun was well up the next morning when we woke to the sound of a sergeant entering the bunker, carrying a clipboard. Evidently, he was making the rounds, seeing that all the generals' stuff was okay, and did not expect to find intruders in foreign uniforms. The feeling of surprise was mutual.

"It's okay—we're Americans!" I blurted. The sergeant appeared unconvinced. I decided to try again.

"We're co-vans—advisors." That didn't seem to cut much ice, either.

"We're Marine majors." That was better. But we still weren't home free. The sergeant gulped and spat it out:

"Sirs—this is the commanding general's bunker. You aren't supposed to be sleeping here."

"We know! We *know!*"

We had reached an impasse. The sergeant backed out, muttering to himself. It did not take long for us to decide that the time was right to look for a helicopter back to An Hoa and not wait for breakfast to be served in the bunker. After all, we had commandeered not just *a* general's bunker; it was *the* general's bunker, and his people might not be good sports about it.

Back at An Hoa, the packup already had begun for the return to Saigon by motor march. Throughout the brigade, hopes were high for a reasonably long stand-down period—long enough for young Marines to return to their homes and families for long-awaited visits. But for Major Tung's troops that hope was short-lived. Within a week, the Sixth Battalion had received orders to move once again, this time to the Ca Mau Peninsula, at the southernmost tip of South Vietnam. Ca Mau was the end of the world, an area unmatched in desolation ever since a massive defoliation effort had stripped bare a great part of its mangrove swamps, leaving a ghostly, ramshackle expanse of large tree trunks, some rising to sixty feet, and bare branches overlooking the tidal floor.

At high tide and during the rainy season, the peninsula is inundated and overland transportation south of Ca Mau City is virtually impossible. The main waterway cutting through the region is the Cua Lon River, a ten-knot river with a ten-foot tidal range. South of the Cua Lon, no one existed but the Vietcong and their families and a few refugees from Nam Can village on the river, destroyed in the wake of the 1968 Tet Offensive.

Despite its atmosphere of desolation and uninhabitability, however, the Cua Lon and its tributaries are rich in seafood, and a tree indigenous to the area produces the finest charcoal in Vietnam. Those two factors were of continuing interest to a variety of powerful forces in the region, constantly seeking economic gain.

The Vietcong were to operate south of the Cua Lon without challenge until mid-1970, because of the difficulty in conducting ground operations to dislodge them. That portion of An Xuyen Province had been exempted from the pacification goals assigned to the commanding general of Military Region IV. In 1968, however, the Commander, U.S. Naval Forces Vietnam, mounted a waterborne challenge by establishing an advanced tactical support base near Nam Can. The base originally consisted of AMMI (named for their inventor, a Dr. Amirikan) pontoon barges lashed together in the middle of the Cua Lon; it provided logistical support for river patrol operations throughout An Xuyen Province. The new asset, called Sea Float, soon became a vulnerability, once the Vietcong began to target this new thorn in their sides. By early 1970, Sea Float had become a matter of mounting concern. No ground attack had yet been launched, but this floating pile of gasoline and ammunition was being targeted by Vietcong sapper swimmers. In one two-month period in the spring of 1970, eight such swimmers, trying to place limpet mines on the barges, were killed by concussion grenades thrown from the barges at random intervals, none more than fifteen minutes long.

The RMK Corporation, tasked with a great deal of military construction throughout Vietnam, was hired to lay down a "seventeen-million dollar sand pile" on the north bank of the Cua Lon, also near Nam Can. It would be the foundation of a 250-by-600-yard cantonment adjacent to a 3,000-foot runway. Its real estate value would rise to seventy-eight million dollars as the SeaBees continued to add improvements (such as a helicopter pad and boat-mooring spaces) and some of the comforts of home (to include electric power and running water). By September 1970, Sea Float was discontinued and all operations were moved ashore to the new base, called Solid Anchor. But the vulnerability to attack had not ended; it merely had changed form.

To counter the threat, a dog's breakfast of dissimilar units had been assembled. In addition to the SeaBees, the base had U.S. and South Vietnamese SEAL teams, noted for their independence, if not outright insubordination; Sea Wolves, who operated the U.S. Navy helicopter gunships; Viet Hai, who in a burst of charity might be described as irregular naval infantry; Vietnamese Special Forces, a collection of thugs whom U.S. advisors had tried unsuccessfully to mold into legitimate Green Berets; U.S. explosive ordnance disposal (EOD) teams, also noted for their free spirits; and Kit Carson Scouts, a euphemism for Vietcong defectors, not exactly objects of special trust and confidence. One bright note in this picture was provided by the Black Ponies, a U.S. Navy light attack squadron flying propeller-driven OV-10 aircraft equipped with rockets and guns, which could provide close air support to troops on the ground.

By midsummer 1970, the Solid Anchor population had grown to more

than six hundred and the melange of forces was conducting (quite) limited offensive operations and manning a defensive perimeter on the north
bank of the Cua Lon. But there were gaps in the defense, such as an inability to fire and service the 81-mm mortars sent to Solid Anchor and a general weakness in controlling all the disparate resident units. To make matters worse, Solid Anchor was essentially unprotected from assault from the
south, where the enemy lived and operated. The Marine Advisory Unit sent
advisors to Solid Anchor to implement a base defense plan and hold 81-
mm mortar school. To correct the second glaring shortfall, the Sixth Battalion got the call: to land by helicopter south of the Cua Lon, then sweep
back toward the south bank of the river and tie into Solid Anchor's defensive perimeter there. The battalion would conduct a two-day motor march
to Ca Mau City, where it would board helicopters for its airborne assault
into the End of the World.

The Solid Anchor advance tactical support base, sitting on the "seventeen-million-
dollar sand pile" at the north bank of the Cua Lon River, overlooks the few
remaining barges of Sea Float, in the middle of the river.

The convoy made an uneventful departure from Saigon and completed the first day's journey without incident, stopping at a roadside village just before sunset. The troops got off the trucks and just melted into the houses and huts closest to the road, without a peep from the residents, as darkness fell. This was a scene difficult to imagine happening in, say, Muncie, Indiana. Was there an intimidation factor present? Quite possibly, but I'm not certain how much of one. I know that I wouldn't have wanted any of those armed men mad at *me*. Major Tung, of course, bunked in with the village chief, in the biggest and best house. And once again, I bedded down on the porch.

The next day, I flew ahead to the U.S. Navy's Mekong Delta headquarters in Binh Thuy to receive an operational briefing on the helicopter assault plan, as the battalion continued its motor march to Ca Mau City. It would be like attending the reunion of a dysfunctional family. This headquarters was the fiefdom of The Admiral—the same admiral the co-vans had eluded in the Great Escape of 30 June. I hoped that The Admiral would not hold a grudge.

But there was yet another complicating factor, co-van-wise, in the person of Bad Jack Maxwell, Major of Marines. Because of the increased interest in Solid Anchor, Jack had been pulled from his enviable position as senior advisor to the Fourth Battalion and placed on The Admiral's staff as a ground plans officer—much like Capt. Bill Healy—and he, also, was a most unhappy camper.

Jack and I had commanded adjacent rifle companies west of Da Nang in 1965. After his Alpha Company got overrun one October night (the event misreported by the California radio station), I asked Jack what it was like to get overrun. "Well," he said, "once you get used to the idea that you're not going to live through it, then you're okay." Jack's somewhat romantic, soldier-of-fortune view of life probably was present all along, but this searing experience certainly brought it to the fore. I next encountered Jack five years later at the Marine Advisory Course at Quantico, and we roomed together for three months while we brushed up on fire-support control skills and tried total immersion in the Vietnamese language.

While at Quantico I loaned Jack a copy of *Never So Few,* a terrific novel about advisors to Burmese guerrillas during World War II, by Tom

Chamales. It was a great preview of the world we were entering, and Jack loved it as much as I did. He gave me back my copy, but when he went home to Camp Pendleton en route to Vietnam, he drove to the base library and checked one out, with no intention of ever returning it. Months later, as the novel passed from advisor to advisor in almost a cult status, Jack wrote to his long-suffering wife at Camp Pendleton and asked her to go to the library and pay for the long-overdue book.

Jack's soldier-of-fortune penchant was served handsomely by his assignment to the Fourth Battalion, the only one not headquartered in Saigon. The Fourth Battalion had been involved in the 1963 coup that led to the assassination of President Diem and his brother-in-law Nhu (in effect, a co-president); they helped storm the Presidential Palace. The South Vietnamese military had been virtually unanimous in supporting the coup, which occurred with the complicity—full knowledge, together with a hands-off attitude—of U.S. officials at the highest level. As a matter of fact, the co-vans at that time had been ordered by senior U.S. officials to go to their Saigon hotel rooms and stay there until the dust settled.

Be that as it may, the Fourth Battalion thereafter was singled out as a pariah organization and banished from Saigon to Vung Tau (the resort town at Cape St. Jacques), in a move somewhat akin to throwing Br'er Rabbit into the briar patch. In the 1960s, there had been fierce fighting in nearby rubber plantations, but with an Australian battalion now operating in the area alongside the VNMC, the Vietcong didn't see much point in contesting that turf, and contacts were few and far between. So Vung Tau was hardly a grueling assignment for these outcasts, whose association with a major historical event had won them a relatively low-stress existence amid relatively plush surroundings.

Bad Jack's unhappiness—at being yanked out of Vung Tau to become a disgruntled staff officer at Binh Thuy—was about to descend to new depths. Shortly after I reached Binh Thuy, The Admiral entered the operations center and Jack began to brief the next day's insert of the Sixth Battalion into the Solid Anchor area. The briefing was moving along well until Jack got to the fire-support part. There was no artillery support available that far south; the operation would commence outside the range of Solid Anchor's few defensive mortars, and the Vietnamese gunners on the swift boats in the Cua Lon were more of a threat to our own troops than to the enemy. So our landing would be covered by the armed helicopters of the Sea Wolves—or so Jack briefed.

"Oh—I forgot to tell you," The Admiral broke in. "The Sea Wolves had to cancel. Another mission took priority."

"Then we have to postpone the operation," Jack said.

"Oh, no—we'll go ahead on schedule."

"But we can't land these troops in the middle of nowhere without fire support. . . ."

"Major—in wartime, sometimes we have to take a calculated risk."

The ugly thought flashed across my mind: Here, in this air-conditioned operations center far from the heat of combat, I had just become the Calculated Risk of the Day. I got ready to hold some school on these folks, who badly needed some. Disregarding forty years' worth of landing force doctrine and common sense, developed over three wars, might seem like a calculated risk back in Binh Thuy, but to foot sloggers literally up to their asses in swampy marsh land, it was incalculable insanity.

But Jack—who probably had faced more combat-related personal risk than anyone else in that room—beat me to it, in dramatic fashion. He turned a bright red and puffed up like a huge toad, so exasperated that he could not speak at first. As he regained his breath, he began to jab his right forefinger in The Admiral's direction, gasping, "You . . . you . . . you. . . ."

Tears were beginning to appear in the corners of Jack's eyes, clenched shut in anger. Abruptly, he spun on his heel and strode out of the operations center and out of the building.

"Stop him!" The Admiral said, in total disbelief.

I caught up with Jack a block away from the building. He was still struggling to regain his composure, and I did the talking:

"Look—we both know this will never go off without air support," I said. "And do you think for one minute that Major Tung will allow his people to land without it? Hell, no! And besides—he doesn't have to. The Admiral can't make him, because he's not in The Admiral's chain of command."

I went on to elaborate, the better to calm Bad Jack. I pointed out that this was not D-Day at Normandy, and The Admiral was not Dwight Eisenhower, betting his landing decision on a tiny window of decent weather. It was not the rainy season, so we didn't have to wait for a dry day. And we didn't have a tactical problem either. "No one really gives a rat's ass if we land tomorrow, or the next day, or next week—just so we eventually get there. Okay? Let's go make another plan," I concluded.

We went back to the operations center, where a curious calm prevailed. The Admiral had left, and his somewhat shaken staff officers had been making some phone calls. One of the calls had been to VAL-4, the light attack squadron that flew the Black Ponies—those wonderfully accurate OV-10 Broncos equipped with rockets and guns that could hit a gnat in the eye, much better than wild area-suppression machine-gun fire from the door gunners of the Sea Wolves. The Ponies would be there for us.

So it was a go. We worked out the final details, and I flew back to Ca Mau City, to rejoin the Sixth Battalion, which was just concluding its two-day motor march. The Ca Mau helicopter pad, where the Sixth Battalion would load for the assault the next morning, was a mile or so out of town. As we approached town by jeep, I became more and more aware of a pungent, eye-watering smell, getting stronger by the second. I was on the verge of asking my Vietnamese driver some extremely personal questions about the state of his dental hygiene when we turned a corner and the source of the odor came into view.

There, drying—rotting, actually—on a hillside were thousands upon thousands of small fish. The townspeople would capture the juices of decomposition and further refine them to make nuoc mam, a universally used sauce that spiced up rice bowls throughout the land. Nuoc mam was usually too much at first for bland American tastes. It took some determined getting used to, but once that happened it became an indispensable part of every meal. It really did wonders for the rice.

But there would be no rice on the menu this evening. On the eve of battle, the Sixth Battalion was having its customary party, with everything but rice. They had not operated in this area before, but they must have known that they would be living in a tidal marsh for the indefinite future, because they partied as if there were no tomorrow.

I wasn't much in the mood. There would be a tomorrow, and it would come soon enough. Later in the evening, I got word from Saigon that Gene Adams had returned from leave and would meet me on the ground at

Solid Anchor, once the helicopter insert was complete. As the Vietnamese Marines swept back toward their eventual defensive perimeter on the south bank of the Cua Lon, we would cross the river in a small boat and confer with Major Tung. Then the hand-over back to Gene would be complete, and I would return to Saigon to become the G-3 (Operations) advisor to the VNMC.

If only everything would go that smoothly, I thought, as I drifted off to sleep.

Chapter 7

The next day brought a succession of happy surprises. We had excellent flying weather for the helicopter assault. The Black Ponies covered the area in a thorough, workmanlike way that evidently was menacing enough to make the Vietcong think twice about contesting the landing zone—as though the onslaught of a battalion of South Vietnamese Marines, in itself, might not have been a compelling producer of second thoughts. Resistance proved to be virtually nil, and the battalion completed its sweep back to its new home in less than two hours. By mid-afternoon, I had conferred with Gene Adams, accompanied him across the river, said good-bye to Major Tung, and returned to Solid Anchor to hitch a helicopter ride back to Saigon.

My six weeks with the Sixth Battalion had given me a good feel for life on the pointy end of the spear. Nevertheless, it still felt good—for a change—to be the co-van who was handing over his maps with a smile on his face. On the other hand, the mood of Gene Adams seemed to darken as we drew closer to his old battalion and his new home. We crossed the river at low tide, when the mud flats were shining forth in their full fetid glory, and Gene must have convinced himself that the Fates had singled him out for cruel and unusual punishment by sentencing him to serve in the mud at the End of the World, after six glorious weeks in Australia. As things were to develop, however, living in the mud would become the least of

Gene's worries. I flew back to Saigon the next day, but I had neither seen nor heard the last of Solid Anchor. Not by a long shot.

Back in Saigon, I knew that I had a lot to learn before taking over as G-3 (Operations) advisor to the South Vietnamese Marine Division. Fortunately, this time, I would be getting a lot more than a beaming smile, a handshake, and a packet of maps. The outgoing G-3 advisor, Maj. George Rivers, enjoyed a solid reputation with the Vietnamese, which helped me a lot in taking hold as he showed me around. George had his own bit of Jack Maxwell's soldier-of-fortune romanticism, tempered by the more down-to-earth qualities of a University of Oklahoma linebacker and the engaging personality of a fraternity rush chairman. George also had his appetites. At his going-away party, the Vietnamese broke their no-rice rule and presented him with a helmet full of rice, thoroughly laced with nuoc mam, his customary fare in the field. The stench was eye-watering, but George ate every grain, washing it down with *Ba Mười Ba*—the old French "33" beer, with its distinct aftertaste of formaldehyde. I truly appreciated

Recently returned to the Sixth Battalion from six weeks' leave in Australia, co-van Maj. Gene Adams surveys his new home—the fetid mud flats on the south bank of the Cua Long River at low tide.

George's energy and enthusiasm in breaking me in, but I was unconvinced that I ever could put away a helmet full of rice.

In theory, my job was to provide operational, planning, and training advice to the assistant chief of staff (G-3) of the Vietnamese Marine Corps. My counterpart, or "buddy," was Lt. Col. Nguyen The Luong, a long-service infantry officer who had worked his way up through company and battalion command in combat. His nickname, "Laughing Larry," was something of a puzzlement, however, because Colonel Luong's demeanor usually was serious to the point of intensity. But he had a sense of humor and could deliver one-liner commentary with a wry smile and a *yit-yit-yit*— more of a giggle than a real laugh. Rumor had it that his nickname arose from a certain delight in the discomfort of others, captured enemy soldiers in particular. (The Germans have a word for it—Schadenfreude.) Nothing in my experience with Luong confirmed or dispelled such a rumor.

In theory, my duties were quite clear, but there was a considerable gulf between theory and reality. In reality, I never had seen the inside of a U.S. Marine regimental or division command post, except as a visitor. I had been a brigade senior advisor for a few weeks in Cambodia, but Luong was too junior for brigade command, which called for a full colonel. On the other hand, all these fine gradations of command-post experience were essentially irrelevant, because the Vietnamese Marines followed the Cult of the Commander. Battalion and brigade commanders essentially ran their own shows, virtually out of their hip pockets, the way U.S. Marine rifle company commanders might do it. In 1965, at the outset of the Americanized Vietnam War, we even had a few U.S. Marine battalion commanders who tried to run things that way—personally on top of every detail of their units' performance, day and night—but to a man they burned out in a haze of exhaustion and irrationality, after a few weeks at most. The effective commanders learned to distribute the burden of command among their staffs, thus factoring twenty to thirty sets of eyes and ears and a fair amount of additional brain power into the equation, with everyone trying to help the commander do his job.

By 1970, however, this notion still had not entered the Vietnamese Marine mind-set, and the full burden still was carried by the commander. If he succeeded he was a hero, even a demigod; if he failed—or even *appeared* to fail—he was a lost soul, almost beneath contempt, as only a fallen deity could be. He might get some advice from his principal staff officers along the way, but all too often even they were winging it, without a full measure of staff activity and analysis to support their calls.

To be fair, anyone comparing the two systems should note that most of the U.S. commander's staff support in combat came from his combat operations center and fire support coordination center, which blended the maneuver of his subordinate and adjacent units with a wide array of artillery, naval gunfire, and close air support. Aside from his division's light artillery, which might or might not be available on call, the Vietnamese commander did not have to worry about any of that—but his U.S. advisor did.

At any rate, it was evident that the Vietnamese Marine headquarters in Saigon had little direct influence on the day-by-day operations of the distant brigade fiefdoms elsewhere in Vietnam and in Cambodia. Rather, they dealt with the Joint General Staff, forwarding reports from the field and taking part in general operational and organizational planning—budgeting and force structure development, for example. My own G-3 section, in fact, had its own share of reporting requirements within the U.S. chain of command. But before long, it became clear that my *real* job in Saigon was to keep my own Senior Marine Advisor (and the Vietnamese Marines) informed about the ebb and flow of their fortunes in the constantly changing, highly political world of the capital city.

This function called for frequent visits to the ornate headquarters of the Joint General Staff, where the U.S. Marine liaison officer could provide early notice of upcoming deployments and an assessment of how the Vietnamese Marines were doing in the eyes of their sister services.

Another stopping place was the sandbagged command center of the U.S. Military Assistance Command, Vietnam—the MACV "Cave"—located at Tan Son Nhut air base. Marine Colonel Anthony "Cold Steel" Walker, wrapping up his third war, ran the center and always was eager to receive any information from our units in the field. In return, there was not much to learn about the status of U.S. operations, because most of our units had left the country, and most of the rest were getting ready to leave. Aside from U.S. naval gunfire, artillery, and air support, the war was rapidly becoming "Vietnamized." On the other hand, the stops at the MACV Intelligence section, also in the Cave, usually were eye-opening, in what they revealed about the Vietcong and North Vietnamese orders of battle. Truly amazing was the way the enemy, seemingly without effort, could form task organizations of up to multi-division strength while on the move, using an austere communications system that was dwarfed by our own.

Much less frequently, I was able to visit the blandly named but highly classified Studies and Observations Group, which practiced war in the shadows with extremely long-range patrols, among other things. It was in the SOG spaces that I heard a radio intercept of the stressed-out North Vietnamese sapper commander who had walked into the Sixth Battalion's company-sized ambush west of An Hoa. That poor devil really *did* think he was surrounded by a full battalion, instead of a rifle company and a Spooky gunship.

In the course of making the rounds through Saigon, I soon learned that the adversaries of the Vietnamese Marines were not limited to those who wore the black pajamas of the Vietcong or the pith helmets of the North Vietnamese Army. The reasons for hostile feelings on the part of the ARVN were unclear; they may have gone back to the VNMC's role in the 1963 coup d'etat or they may have been rooted in jealousy over the Vietnamese Marines' status as part of the elite National Reserve forces, along with the Airborne and the Rangers. These units were not bound to specific pieces of turf, as the ARVN divisions were, but instead served as "fire brigade" troops, deployed on short notice anywhere in Vietnam or adjacent territory when crises arose. In terms of quality of personnel, equipment, training, and aggressive spirit, too, they quite properly were the subject of widespread envy.

In any event, reports from the field would work their way up through the ARVN chain of command, always through the back door (from somebody's executive officer to the next higher echelon's operations officer, rather than from commander to commander, for example). Such reports would cite curious, irregular periods of Vietnamese Marine inactivity, presumably indicating a lack of fighting spirit. Fortunately for us, a U.S. Marine officer working in the MACV Cave was in a position to waylay these messages just before they reached the highest level of command and provide bootleg copies to us, just in time to have answers ready for the defamatory charges the minute they hit. It did not take long for a pattern to emerge: If the cited period of inactivity was, say, 3 September to 8 October, we invariably found that the Vietnamese Marines had been in a major fight on 2 September and had inflicted heavy casualties on the enemy, who could not muster enough nerve to challenge the VNMC until 9 October, when they promptly got their butts kicked again.

To add insult to attempted injury, the MACV headquarters refused to accept Marine Advisory Unit evaluations of VNMC combat readiness. MACV staff officers kept insisting that the Vietnamese Airborne and Rangers were more highly trained. That dubious contention would be severely challenged under fire a few months later.

After a few unsuccessful attempts with these ploys, the ARVN tried another tack. We received word that the Vietnamese Country Plan was being rewritten and that the Vietnamese Marines were in danger of being downgraded from the elite National Reserve to the status of a territorial ARVN division. Evidently, the VNMC's prowess in battle meant nothing to the myopic Army planners, who were fighting a separate war of their own. Fortunately, the long-range planning section at MACV was headed by a U.S. Navy captain, who accepted our invitation to spend a day with the Marine division. We briefed on the complete sixteen-year battle history of the Vietnamese Marines, then took him out to our recruit training facility at Thu Duc to see our re-creation of the Parris Island boot camp. At the end of that glorious day, the captain said, "You're safe for another five years or so." Too bad for the brave old Army team that really tried on this one, and came so close.

Ironically, the captain's comment would prove to be prophetic. But in 1975, foreclosure proceedings on the Vietnamese Marines would be held by the North Vietnamese Army, not the U.S. and South Vietnamese armies.

After we got the daytime rounds under control, George Rivers set about showing me Saigon by night. Dinner was always available at the Splendid Hotel, home of the co-vans, but that was rather a dismal choice when compared to dining at the Brinks Hotel or any of the others around the city that had rooftop restaurants. All one could get on the Splendid roof was a nasty sunburn during the day. The Brinks, on the other hand, had an acceptable menu, adult beverages, and movies after dinner for the less adventuresome.

For the more adventuresome, the blandishments of Saigon, the Pearl of the Orient, were no farther away than Le Loi Street, just a few blocks away. The first stop often was the Hoa Binh ("Peace") bar, which also carried its old "*La Paix*" sign for any die-hard Francophiles who might be walking by. By anyone's standard, the Hoa Binh was a hole in the wall, whose unpretentious exterior was matched only by its unpretentious interior. The bar itself started about halfway down the long, narrow room on the left and did not leave much space for tables and chairs. On a good night there always was a standing-room-only crowd, which the patrons seemed to like. One of its main attractions was the guitar player behind the bar, who could play music from around the world as well as Vietnamese and American songs. One of his better offerings was a rendition of "Malageña Salerosa," a love song dedicated to the women of Malaga, allegedly Spain's most beautiful.

For quite a while, the Hoa Binh had been the favored watering spot of the Vietnamese Airborne Division and their advisors, and in their absence during the Cambodian incursion, beginning in April 1970, it was adopted by increasing numbers of Vietnamese Marines and their co-vans, either based in Saigon or passing through. When the incursion began to wind down and the return of the paratroopers to Saigon was imminent, there was a slight bit of concern: Would they try to make a turf fight of it and attempt to reclaim their old haunt? Stranger things had been known to happen in barrooms filled with aggressive, physically fit males. By this time, two brigades worth of co-vans were back from Cambodia, in addition to the usual Hoa Binh patrons. The only thing to do was to go down there in force and find out.

On the fateful evening a larger contingent of co-vans than usual descended on the Hoa Binh from the Splendid, the Brinks, and other dinner sites. The paratroopers were already there, in strength. The co-vans burst through the door, and for a tense moment the two groups sniffed each other out, like two large dogs, each uncertain of the other's intentions. Then somebody said, "Have a beer!" and the ice was broken. The brothers-in-arms merged for a grand party, with standees three or four deep at the bar, just the way everyone liked it. Individuals would take turns buying the beer, working their way up to the bar, buying four or five beers at a time, keeping one, and passing the others back into the crowd. Then they would melt back into the crowd to receive their just rewards whenever they ran dry.

For most, an evening at the Hoa Binh was satisfying enough in itself; but for those who desired even later evening entertainment, The Pink Pussycat and Mimi's Flamboyant Bar, Lounge, and Restaurant were particular co-van favorites, especially after the 10:00 p.m. curfew for all Americans, including the co-vans. As a matter of official policy, known to all disgruntled MACV staffers of all services, a curfew violation would result in a DR (discrepancy report) which, when noted on the officer's next report of fitness, could wipe out a full year of hard work in the Cave. Unofficially, however, because co-vans were constantly rotating between Saigon and the field, the Senior Marine Advisor saw no point in curtailing their liberty while in town, especially since Saigon after dark was considerably safer than, say, Washington, D.C., at any hour. He would read the DRs, of course, looking—usually in vain—for some truly interesting discrepancies. But eventually he consigned them to the circular file.

On the Vietnamese side, the co-vans were covered by instructions from the Commandant of the Vietnamese Marine Corps to the white-shirted National Police, the "White Mice": "These are my boys. If they are not doing anything wrong, don't mess with them," or words to that effect. Reportedly, these first were written instructions, with a copy carried by each co-van. After a while, however, this became unnecessary; the White Mice not only recognized the Marine tiger suits but also seemed to be able to pick out the co-vans on liberty in civilian clothes, and would leave them alone.

On rare occasions, when things were perhaps a bit more tense than usual, a Vietnamese Marine driver might be found trailing his co-van, and any others in the area, through the nearly deserted streets of late-night Saigon, at a respectful distance, a block or so back. These drivers, who doubled as bodyguards, were accomplished in the martial arts and occasionally got to use their skills. Jack Maxwell's driver *Hạ-sĩ* (Corporal) Quan, a pock-marked little devil who weighed barely a hundred pounds soaking wet, once encountered a six-foot-tall American, wearing a tiger suit. Not recognizing him as one of the co-vans, Quan politely asked the American where he had obtained the suit and was told rather impolitely to buzz off— something a real co-van would never do. Left with little choice, Quan promptly knocked the big guy cold. Then he dumped him into the back of his jeep and drove him over to the Bo Tu Lenh headquarters complex, where his status as a non-co-van was confirmed immediately. After additional checking, the American was identified as a deserter from the U.S. Army and was promptly turned over to Army officials for the next stage of his personal adventure.

Corporal Quan, jeep driver for the Fourth Battalion's senior co-van, once kayoed and took into custody a six-foot-tall American deserter for unauthorized wearing of the Marine tiger suit and for unmannerly conduct.

For the more sedate liberty hounds, the music clubs were a unique feature of Saigon night life. Perhaps the best-known of these was Joe Marcel's on Le Loi Street, whose lead singer was Le Thu, the South Vietnamese equivalent of Peggy Lee. Her trademark was a big, brass medallion dangling from her neck, no matter what her costume of the evening happened to be. Other singers would turn up at Joe Marcel's at regular intervals during the evening, making a circuit of several clubs and restaurants on any given night. Most singers came with highly personalized slide shows flashing on the wall behind them as they sang: standing in various gardens, the Saigon Zoo, or other spots of beauty and looking pensively out to the horizon. The patrons had a choice: They could stay in one place and hear a variety of acts throughout the evening, or pick a favorite singer and follow her (or him) from club to club all evening—a sure way to tire of the slide show, if not the singing.

The popular songs in South Vietnam at that time were ballads that tended to be melodious, sad, and intensely personal. One evening in Joe Marcel's, a reasonably young-looking man got up to sing a somebody-done-somebody-wrong song, without benefit of slide show. It was about a young man who had gone off to war, buoyed by his sweetheart's promise to wait faithfully for his return. When he came home, grievously wounded and emotionally shattered by his battlefield experience, he learned that his intended had run off with a civilian who was making big bucks on the Saigon black market. The audience seemed to hang on every note, and as my eyes became accustomed to the dim, multi-colored lighting I could see scars on the singer's cheeks just below his dark glasses, and I could see the empty right sleeve of his jacket, pinned up. Later that evening, I was able to piece the story together. The singer was indeed singing his own personal song. He had been grievously wounded in battle and had been awarded the Vietnamese equivalent of the Medal of Honor. Everyone in the room knew all this because they knew him, they knew his girl friend, and they knew the civilian she had run off with—personally. Powerful stuff, this.

The singers at Joe Marcel's were not averse to extending their emotional umbrella to Americans. When one co-van, a regular patron when he was in town, made his final appearance there before catching his Freedom Bird back to the United States, Le Thu dedicated a special song to him: Barry

Sadler's "Ballad of the Green Berets." It did not matter that Sadler had written his ballad about the U.S. Army's Special Forces. To these Vietnamese, the green beret meant only one thing: the Vietnamese Marines.

No description of Saigon nights would be complete without mention of the Bong Lai, an upscale Chinese restaurant downtown that was the place to celebrate special occasions. Aside from its exquisite menu, the Bong Lai's most outstanding feature was its house band. All of the musicians were Vietnamese, except for the string bass player, who was the spitting image of Charles de Gaulle, height and all. It was enough to set one wondering if young Major or Lieutenant Colonel de Gaulle had served any time at all in Vietnam before World War II began in earnest.

One evening at the Bong Lai stands out vividly. It was the birthday of Co (Miss) Ninh, who tended bar at the Splendid Hotel and thus was a co-van favorite. We told her that we wanted to take her to the Bong Lai for her birthday dinner party. Tactfully, she explained to us the Vietnamese custom that the person celebrating the birthday was required to pay the full freight for any dining or entertainment, and therefore, she would cover the bill. We replied that this was an American party, that Vietnamese customs did not apply, and that she was evermore our guest. At the restaurant, one of the co-vans—who, with the unlikely name of Sean Carmine Del Grosso, happened to be fluent in Mandarin Chinese—overheard some of the Chinese waiters plotting to shame Co Ninh into paying for her birthday dinner quietly, after the advisors had settled the bill. They then would distribute the extra payment among themselves. Sean began to berate them vigorously in Chinese, settling into an Imperial Whine, rising in pitch and decibels to truly terrifying dimensions, as ancient peasants must have felt when confronted by a warlord who was in a mood to make heads roll. By the time Sean had finished with them, the waiters probably would have been willing to pay him out of their own pockets, if he only would stop the raving and go away, but we settled up and left.

Maybe we should have stayed and made the waiters pay. After we learned some of the tricks of Saigon nights, we got fairly good at spotting those who were out to cheat U.S. servicemen. And thanks to our tiger suits, they could see us coming. Their refrain almost became universal: "You Cheap Charlie, you come in here, nobody smile."

On the first day of October, the Vietnamese Marines celebrated their sixteenth birthday. After a stirring ceremony at Thu Duc, where decorations were awarded for recent combat operations, that evening's birthday party was, in the most charitable sense of the word, lame. Preliminary planning for our own 195th birthday on 10 November already was under way, but after a hurried conference the decision was made to escalate, for purposes of instruction as well as entertainment. We would throw a full-fledged Marine Corps Birthday Ball, just like the ones that would be going on throughout the United States (some twelve hours after ours) and every other clime and place in the world where our Marines were stationed. We would bring the full magic of the evening to our buddies at their Song Thang officers' club, with its beautiful swimming pool adjacent to the dance floor. We would have a cake-cutting ceremony, and promptly sent off to Da Nang for a set of Marine Corps colors and some sheet music for the Marines' Hymn. On their first go-around with the music, the Vietnamese bandsmen sounded like Herb Alpert's "Tijuana Taxi," a couple of quarts low. But musicians are musicians the world over, and before long they were playing their way into the Halls of Montezuma in fine style. And we also would dine in fine style, after sending down to the Mekong Delta for some lobster-like shellfish and hitting up the U.S. Army's bellyrobbers for some steaks, which would be sliced down to filets to fit Vietnamese sensibilities. Then we sent handwritten invitations to all the Vietnamese officers and their ladies.

With nearly everything in place, we waited for replies to the invitations. And waited. And waited. Several days went by. Not a single reply. With mounting frustration, Colonel Tief, the senior advisor, paid a call on Colonel Que, the Vietnamese Marine Corps chief of staff. Tentatively, and as directly as he dared, he asked:

"Why have your officers not responded to our invitations?"

"We did not know what you meant. They were addressed to 'Officers and their Ladies.'"

On National Day, 1 November 1970, Vietnamese Marines are brought front and center to receive decorations for heroism in battle.

"Well . . . ?"

"We did not know whether you meant our wives or our girlfriends."

"*Well . . . ?*"

"Well, if you don't care which, I will make a decision. Our wives will make the party official, but the girlfriends are more fun, because they know all the latest dances. So the senior officers will attend with their wives, to make the party official. They will stay for the cake-cutting and official ceremonies, then depart—leaving the junior officers and their girl-friends to continue the party. At that point, it will become an American party, so Madame Nhu's prohibition of dancing in Saigon during wartime will no longer apply. That should make everyone smile."

The Birthday Ball was on! And the co-vans couldn't wait to see the interaction between the wives and girlfriends when they first confronted each other. Surely, daggers would be flying across the dance floor. Angry words might be exchanged. Hair might be pulled. But once again, reality intruded. The wives and the girlfriends were comfortable in their respective stations in life. The wives knew that they were the official ones, who could wear the formal *ao dai* outfits and talk among themselves about babies and diapers with impunity because their presence gave the party status in polite society. On the other hand, the girlfriends, twitching impatiently in their mini-skirts waiting for the music to begin, were secure in the knowledge that they were more fun.

After the confrontation that never happened, the birthday evening unfolded in generally predictable fashion, except for the dramatic arrival of several co-vans from distant provinces. Capt. Butch Neal won the grand prize by getting a running start and sliding across the dance floor on his knees—muddy boots and all—announcing his arrival from the north.

After the last dance was finished, the co-vans moved on to the Marine House downtown, where Capt. Herb Steigleman and his embassy guards were holding a jubilant block party with a couple thousand of their nearest and dearest that lasted until the dawn's early light. As the small-town society columnists would say, a good time was had by all. I just hoped that the North Vietnamese were not taking notes and planning a major offensive for the same time next year.

Chapter 8

As the fall days got shorter, though not particularly cooler, in Saigon, Vietnamese Marine units began to return from Cambodia. After some rest and refitting, some of the battalions moved northward to a new area of operations along the Demilitarized Zone, the laughably named DMZ, which had been the scene of some of the war's heaviest fighting in the late 1960s, when the U.S. Marines operated there.

Then, after a few weeks along the "Zee," the Americans had become more or less permanently reddened by constant contact with the clay soil found throughout the region; their boots, their uniforms, their skin, their hair and eyebrows, and even their eyes turned an orangeish red. But the Vietnamese Marines, accustomed to the warmth of the Mekong Delta and Cambodia, had a different problem. On higher ground, much farther north, as the fall monsoon eased into the damp chill of winter, the South Vietnamese tended to turn blue. Whenever the temperature dipped below 70 degrees, they were in trouble, especially at night. The hours could drag on seemingly without end for anyone curled up in a poncho, waiting . . . waiting . . . waiting for the first warming rays of the sun. These Middle Region Blues were similar to those faced a few months earlier by the Vietnamese Marines in Operation Vu Ninh XII, west of Da Nang and An Hoa, only more so.

This was not a universal condition within the Vietnamese Marine Division just yet, however. Maj. Jack Maxwell, his services no longer needed by The Admiral in Binh Thuy once the Solid Anchor insert of the Sixth Battalion had been completed, had returned to his own Fourth Battalion in its hardship resort base camp at Vung Tau. As the G-3 advisor, I needed first-hand knowledge of the morale, discipline, and leadership in all our battalions, and I was only too happy to accept Jack's invitation for a three-day visit to Vung Tau, roughly a two-hour jeep ride from Saigon.

On my first day there, we drove through a rubber plantation that had been the scene of heavy fighting a few years earlier, now patrolled by an Australian infantry battalion. Then, as dusk fell, we went into town. I had a room at the only hotel in town, named (with typical Vietnamese understatement) the Grand Hotel. At least it was grander and more splendid than the Splendid Hotel in Saigon. After dinner there, we retired to the small but tastefully appointed bar, complete with trademark overhead fans spinning lazily in the best Raffles of Singapore fashion. Jack and I picked a table. The place was practically empty, except for two very large Australian soldiers standing at the bar, each with a mug of beer firmly in hand. The Aussies had a 10:00 p.m. curfew, too—just like the one in Saigon—and a few minutes before the witching hour, a sergeant stuck his head through the door and announced in a loud, clear voice:

"Ten minutes, mytes!"

This clarion call evidently surprised one of the Diggers at the bar, who could only respond with a disgusted "Aargh. . . ."

This response proved to be more of a challenge to the sergeant than anyone might have suspected. A squat, powerful man, built like a fire hydrant, he pushed his way into the bar. He walked up to the bigger of the two Aussie troopers and delivered his ultimatum:

"You, myte—you've got ten seconds!"

The trooper took down his beer in three gulps, well ahead of the ten-second limit. Then he and his buddy left the bar immediately, without further incident.

Now, *that's* discipline. Even while acknowledging that the scene might have been staged to impress us, we were duly impressed.

For the second evening in Vung Tau, Jack arranged a dinner with the chief of police, at a local restaurant. We had a delightful chicken dinner, washed down with the ubiquitous Ba Muoi Ba beer. Per custom, we cooled the beer with ice cubes in the glass; watering that particular beer was not a bad idea. It was a pleasant, friendly meal, followed by a tour of the town, personally guided by the chief of police and punctuated by his insightful remarks about what really went on there. As we parted, it was easy to decline his heartfelt offer of a woman for the evening—not only on general principles, but also because I was getting about ready to explode and needed to return to my room in the Grand Hotel.

Jack and I got back there just in time. The explosion came from both ends, and I eventually found refuge in a four-legged bathtub, where I could be cooled and washed down as needed. By dawn, the explosions had stopped, the fever seemed to have been broken, and I could crawl out of the Grand Hotel's bathtub into Jack's jeep for a trip to the local military dispensary, run by the Air Force. After the hellishness of the preceding evening, I felt absolutely cool, but my temperature still was running about 103 degrees. Jack dumped me back into his jeep and began the drive back to Saigon. I was deposited in my room in the Splendid, and the Marine Advisory Unit's doctor stopped by once a day to monitor my progress or at least to make sure I was still alive. After a truly out-of-body experience for a week or so, I was able to return to full duty, feeling as though I had been dragged through a knothole.

What caused this? It probably wasn't the food, which was as well prepared as anything in Saigon. And the Ba Muoi Ba embalming fluid we drank certainly could not have harbored any alien bacteria for more than a millisecond. So it must have been the ice we used to cool the beer. One of the icehouses must have obtained it from other-than-authorized rice paddies. Or maybe I hadn't built up enough Vung Tau–specific antibodies, because Bad Jack and the chief of police drank the same beer with the same melted ice without noticeable effect. At any rate, the experience was almost enough to make someone stop putting ice in his beer.

After I recovered, I didn't get another chance to see if I now had become immune to Vung Tau ice, because Bad Jack and the Fourth Battalion moved north to join the growing Vietnamese Marine presence along the

DMZ. Contact with North Vietnamese units in the area was only sporadic at the time. However, Jack's assistant advisor, Capt. Scrap Harrell, got nicked badly enough in one firefight to be evacuated to a U.S. Army field hospital at the nearby Dong Ha combat base. (It somewhat resembled the Korean War medical facilities made famous by *M*A*S*H*.) Dong Ha, the center of operations for some fifty thousand U.S. Marines just two years earlier, was in the process of being dismantled as part of the accelerating U.S. effort to pull its forces out of the war.

After a week or so, Jack decided that it was time to check on Scrap, to ensure that he was receiving proper care and attention. At dusk one evening, he took a fifth of whiskey and a jeep and bounced eastward along National Highway 9 to Dong Ha, a journey of perhaps ten kilometers. Oblivious to mines, enemy patrols, jittery friendly sentries, and other things that might go bang in the night, he arrived at the hospital area unscathed. In no time he had found Scrap's tent and had broken out the bottle to stimulate some earnest conversation. Scrap joined in with enthusiasm, and as the bottle emptied and the mood mellowed toward a deep delta-wave stage, Jack concluded that Scrap was just about cured and quite ready to rejoin the battalion, no matter what the medics said. What did they know about the physical demands of combat, anyway? Bunch of rear-echelon pukes, they were.

At precisely this point in Jack's emotional excursion, a U.S. Army hospital duty officer with an exquisitely horrible sense of timing entered the tent while making his rounds of the wards. And what to his wondering eyes did appear but a large, unkempt, unshorn, unshaven individual in a red-clay-stained spiky-camouflaged foreign uniform. The intruder obviously was threatening the hygienic well-being of one of his patients, so the duty medical officer spoke out, in a way that made Jack feel unwelcome. This may have been called for by hospital procedure, but it was clearly a tactical mistake.

Challenging Jack in adversarial circumstances would have been a mistake; challenging him in a convivial mood was an even bigger mistake, because that would constitute a personal betrayal. In any event, Jack swiftly made the duty officer feel unwelcome; indeed, he made the duty officer go away. After a minute's consideration of the resulting wreckage,

Jack hoisted Scrap over his shoulder and left the scene—back to the jeep, Route 9, and all the dangers thereof.

Obviously, this sudden disappearance into the darkness was a violation of normal hospital check-out procedure. In assessing the situation the next morning, the quasi-*M*A*S*H* officials had much to contend with. Not only was a patient unaccounted for, but also they had no inkling of where to find him in the morass of Vietnamese units just outside their lines. So they decided to prepare a report—a scathing report. Then they drew straws to see which of the young doctors would carry it to Saigon, to initiate the search for the unidentified foreign-uniformed intruder.

Getting from Dong Ha to Saigon was no easy matter. The trip began at the Dong Ha helicopter landing pad, where one waited for a lift to Phu Bai. With luck, a traveler could catch a fixed-wing airlift from Phu Bai to Da Nang, which boasted a much larger air terminal. Then, from Da Nang, in time, a flight in a larger aircraft to Tan Son Nhut airfield in Saigon could be boarded on a space-available basis. Smooth connections were by no means certain. But the doctor carrying the medical report would be able to enjoy at least a day or two in Saigon before returning to Dong Ha, where his services were always in demand.

The young doctor with the winning straw was waiting patiently at the Dong Ha helipad, undoubtedly thinking of the good life in Saigon, when he was approached by another waiting passenger. The second man at the pad was Capt. Steve Lindblom, a co-van also en route to Saigon. Steve had been hardened in the field, with an earlier successful combat tour (a prerequisite for service as a co-van) as a rifle company commander. But he was blessed, or cursed, with a youthful countenance that could express such wonderment, on call, that it brought him the sobriquet of "L'il Stevie Wonder."

Steve, as it happened, had heard the story from Jack Maxwell and knew quite well why a doctor might be on his way to Saigon at this particular time. But he asked him anyway.

The doctor promptly spilled his guts.

Stevie Wonder assumed The Look: "Oh, that's awful," he said, going on to lament the great shame and embarrassment brought on all their heads by the miscreant in the tiger suit, whom, he assured the doctor, they had been tracking for months. "Now we can nail him! I tell you what—give me that report! I am going to Saigon anyway, and I can deliver it directly to the Senior Marine Advisor, who can hunt him down." He turned a clear inno-cent gaze to the doctor, all eager concern. "You don't have any other real reason to go to Saigon, do you?"

The doctor hesitated, conscience-stricken. He knew that they needed him more in Dong Ha than in Saigon, and that others might die while he played, if he went on to Saigon.

"No. I think you can improve things more than I can . . . ."

Stevie Wonder was a man of his word. He delivered the report directly to the Senior Marine Advisor, in person. The Senior Marine Advisor promptly read it and smiled, no doubt wondering, "Where do we get such men?" Then, he placed it on the corner of his desk, atop the stack of the current week's discrepancy reports from the military police in Saigon, usually guaranteed to produce a few grins.

As the fall deepened, we began to hear rumbles from Solid Anchor. The U.S. Navy commander of that advanced tactical support base on the Cua Lon River was running into problems. Reportedly, he had been an exchange student at the U.S. Army's Command and General Staff College, but nothing he learned at Fort Leavenworth could have prepared him to lead the conglomeration of disparate units and individuals—all carrying the poisonous short-timer's attitude—collected at Solid Anchor.

Despite such creature comforts as electricity and running water installed by the SeaBees, the base was considered a hardship post, and tours there were limited to ninety days, except for key command and staff positions and the Vietnamese Marine battalion guarding against ground attack from the south. Such a constant turnover of personnel just about guaranteed low levels of military proficiency and knowledge of the watery terrain and the enemy. Moreover, there was not much promise of quick learning by new arrivals, each of whom hung up his individualized version of a ninety-day short-timer's calendar and marked off Day One as his first order of business.

We were hearing rumbles of intense mutual dislike between the base's executive officer and the Vietnamese inhabitants, which had led to a demonstration in the mess hall by many Vietnamese banging their metal trays on the mess tables, a trick they no doubt had learned by watching old American prison movies. We also were getting reports that Major Tung and his high-flying Sixth Battalion were growing restive in the stinking mud flats at the End of the World. It was time for the Senior Marine Advisor to see for himself. We had to go down there and take a look.

The Innkeepers, our favorite Army heavy-lift helicopter squadron, provided one of their command birds, an OH-58 Kiowa, to fly us down to Solid Anchor and back to Saigon, about two hours each way on this single-day trip. Col. Bui The Lan, the Assistant Commandant of the Vietnamese Marines, would accompany Colonel Tief and me, to take a close look at the Sixth Battalion and the overall setup.

There was a continuing love-in between the co-vans and the Innkeepers, based on mutual appreciation of military skills and a shared fierce protectiveness. The U.S. Army pilots knew that the co-vans would not try to make life easier for themselves by bringing the choppers in to hot landing zones, and the advisors knew that those pilots would break flight-hour restrictions or anything else that kept them from giving the Vietnamese Marines the support they needed when they needed it. Whenever an Innkeeper traveled to Saigon from his base in Can Tho, he was wined and dined like a returning prodigal; the same thing happened to co-vans bound for destinations in the Mekong Delta, who managed to go through Can Tho while en route. To be ready for an early takeoff, our pilot for the Solid Anchor trip had flown into Saigon the preceding evening, in time to receive the customary four-star treatment, which in turn kept him from being truly ready for an early-morning takeoff.

This was not evident as I slid into the co-pilot's space in our four-seater Kiowa, but shortly after we had been cleared for takeoff and lifted out of Tan Son Nhut airfield, the pilot took on a look of sudden fatigue. Clearly, he was undergoing a massive sinking spell and wanted some more sleep—immediately.

"Ever flown one of these before?" he asked, almost too casually.

"Well, no—I'm a grunt."

"Would you like to?"

"Well, sure—what do you have to do?"

"It's easy. You just have to work the stick and the pedals. Stay on this course at this altitude, all the way in to Solid Anchor. If you see any thunderstorms ahead, go around them, not through them. That's about all. There's no terrain to worry about. The Delta is one big flat landing zone."

"Why the hell not?"

"Attaboy. I need some shuteye. Wake me when it's time to talk to the tower at Solid Anchor, and I'll take her in for the landing."

For the next two hours, I was in hog heaven. Staying on course was easy, and after a bit of experimentation, I was able to settle on a stick-and-pedal combination that smoothed out a mild roller-coaster ride into a fairly level flight at the required altitude. I just hoped that the pilot wasn't too heavy a sleeper, requiring extraordinary measures to awaken.

Shortly after we landed at Solid Anchor, our worst suspicions were confirmed. The gloom of self-pity that enveloped the base was thick enough to cut with a knife. The variety of uniforms and pieces of uniforms was staggering, and many men were walking around without either shirts or military headgear, making it impossible to determine either their units or their rank. It was difficult to determine how the base was organized. If anyone wanted to get a boat to cross the Cua Lon River, he had to find the lance corporal with the keys, instead of going to the N-4 or logistic section and obtaining both a boat and an operator. Except for the Combat Operations Center, which had round-the-clock watch-standers, the base did not seem to have a pattern of working hours, where individuals were expected to be at their appointed places of duty. The relationship between the executive officer and the Vietnamese in Solid Anchor seemed every bit as poisonous as rumored, but things appeared to be under control for now. It was across the river, with Major Tung's Sixth Battalion, where things were about ready to explode.

Things had gone downhill since the Sixth Battalion's helicopter insert, and Major Tung was growing more alienated from the Solid Anchor operation each day. The swamp-like living conditions were made worse on occasions when Vietnamese Navy river patrol boats, as part of their defenses at night, would fire randomly in a 360-degree arc at the river banks, with some rounds hitting inside the Vietnamese Marine positions. Tung's bitter complaints brought no end to this totally unprofessional and reckless practice. Shortly before we arrived that very day, the U.S. Navy SEAL detachment commander had responded with insulting language to something that Major Tung had said, even though he clearly was Tung's junior. As I had learned in my six weeks with him, Tung took matters of seniority quite seriously, and this lack of deference from a junior officer had sent his aristocratic sensibilities into overdrive. He was fit to be tied.

After severe pressure from Colonel Tief, the SEAL commander had agreed to cross the river and apologize to Major Tung face to face. He was just getting into the boat when an electrifying report came in from the Combat Operations Center. The duty officer there had not stayed on top of friendly positions on the situation map and had cleared a Sea Wolf helicopter in hot for a strafing run against what turned out to be Sixth Battalion positions. Six Vietnamese Marines died in the attack, and twelve were wounded. Tung's rage was boundless. Even the conciliatory Gene Adams could not dampen it. If the SEAL officer tried to smooth over anything after this, he would be lucky to get back alive. We canceled the make-amends trip across the river.

Colonel Lan, Colonel Tief, and I boarded the helicopter for the return flight to Saigon with some troubling thoughts. Both Major Tung and Solid Anchor's commanding officer seemed to be nearing the end of their respective ropes. We had seen other Vietnamese commanders radicalized into rigid anti-American mind-sets, with devastating personal consequences for the unfortunate co-vans assigned to them. In one instance, the advisor had hunkered down and weathered all the slights and abuses thrown his way with a display of fortitude and character that finally—after most of a year—had put his counterpart to shame. The Vietnamese officer broke down, cried, and begged for forgiveness. Not every situation had so happy an ending, though. The prospects for the Sixth Battalion and its co-vans were not pleasant to contemplate.

Once in the air, our Innkeeper pilot, looking much more rested than early that morning, asked if I wanted to fly the helicopter back to Saigon. Evidently, he figured that a little more rest would prepare him well for the entertainments of Saigon that night. That was fine with me. I kept the stick until it was time to talk to Tan Son Nhut, and he hovered, taxied, and landed. As we climbed out of the aircraft, I spoke to Colonel Lan.

"Did you enjoy your flight?"

Lan's eyes narrowed. He was a highly intelligent man and knew that a helicopter has the flight characteristics of a boulder. He also knew that helicopters were held up in the sky only by brute mechanical force and thousands of moving parts, any one of which could fail without notice, bringing catastrophic results.

"Yes," he said, wondering what was coming next.

"Good—because I was your pilot."

Lan's eyes darted quickly to my left breast pocket, looking for flying wings. But the only wings sewn on there were for *jumping,* out of perfectly good airplanes. The echo of " . . . I was your pilot" seemed to be reverberating through his brain housing group, as he struggled to make sense of the totally absurd.

This was not the reaction I had anticipated. But Colonel Tief broke the impasse with a short laugh:

"I *knew* something funny was going on in front. Except for the takeoffs and landings, it felt like we kept skidding sideways through the air!"

Chapter 9

It did not take long for the simmering Solid Anchor to boil over. Major Tung turned his perimeter defense south of the Cua Lon into a separate encampment. He accepted no Vietnamese visitors from Solid Anchor and permitted none of his officers and men to visit the tactical support base. The Vietnamese Navy boats continued their haphazard operations, carrying out mission orders only when it suited them and still firing at random into areas held by friendly forces. The SEALs continued to act with an unwarranted spirit of independence. And mounting tensions between the Vietnamese and Americans on base exploded when some Vietnamese explosive ordnance demolitionists assaulted three SeaBees and had to be sent back to Saigon for disciplinary action.

The despair of Solid Anchor's commanding officer gradually deepened to the point where he felt compelled to call the Commander, Naval Forces Vietnam, and request his own relief—thus ending his promising naval career. The only thing worse than involuntary relief of a combat command is relief of the entirely voluntary sort, in the cold-eyed view of boards charged with selecting the best-qualified officers for promotion.

ComNavForV did not waste any time. After filling the gap with the Senior Naval Advisor from Saigon, the three-star admiral cast about for a commander who was competent to run ground operations, in addition to Solid Anchor's basic mission of supporting the naval riverine forces. The choice—at least for long enough to get the base up and running again—was obvious: Colonel Frank Tief, the Senior Marine Advisor. The choice would be precedent-setting. As far as anyone knew, Colonel Tief would be the first U.S. Marine to take command of a Navy combat-support activity in wartime, and the first advisor ever to take command at a level directly over a Vietnamese unit. If any senior naval officers in country found this off-putting, none of them raised objections at the time. There were no volunteers among them for the job, which already had killed one naval career. So be it.

Before he left Saigon, Colonel Tief called on Lieutenant General Khang, the Vietnamese Marine commandant. Khang was adamant: "Do not go down there! I know those bastards down there. They will try to hurt you!" But the die was cast.

On his way south, Tief spent three days visiting Army advisory units in the Delta, accompanied by their senior advisor, John Paul Vann, one of our most experienced Vietnam hands, well versed in the intrigues of state. Vann also was worried:

"Frank, you will be stepping on a lot of toes down there just by showing up," he said. "Watch your ass. I mean it!"

For a much-needed operations assistant at Solid Anchor, Colonel Tief took Capt. Marshall Carter, who had been serving as my assistant in the G-3 shop at the Bo Tu Lenh. Marsh, like Ted Bierman and Gene Adams, was a fourth-generation West Pointer. His father had served as Gen. George C. Marshall's executive assistant after World War II and had retired as a three-star general, commanding the signals interceptors and code-breakers at the National Security Agency at Fort Meade, Maryland.

General Marshall's numerous and spectacular wartime and peacetime accomplishments (as Secretary of Defense and Secretary of State) tended to mask the fact of his deeply felt hatred toward the U.S. Marine Corps. Dating from World War I and carried past World War II, it fueled an unsuccessful attempt to destroy the Corps through executive fiat in the late 1940s. Imagine the consternation in the Carter (and Marshall) families, when, barely a decade later, young Marshall Carter opted for a Marine Corps career after graduating from West Point. The idea!

As many who come from such high-powered backgrounds are, Marsh was tightly strung. But instead of being strung with violin strings of catgut, Marsh was strung with wires of steel, like a Steinway grand piano. Marsh could endure a great deal of pounding and still stay focused and in tune with what needed to be done. In an earlier tour as a rifle company commander in Vietnam, his intense focus on the objective and total disregard for his own safety had brought him the Navy Cross, outranked only by the Medal of Honor in our nation's awards for valor and intrepidity in combat.

Tief and Carter were just what Solid Anchor needed. Frank Tief was a man of imaginative, wide-ranging ideas; Marsh Carter was the steely-eyed executive officer—or executioner, as often was to be the case. As a first priority they established working hours, when everyone had to be out of his rack and doing something useful, as opposed to off-duty hours, when only the watch-standers had to be out of their racks and doing something useful.

Next they established a uniform, to help identify all the stray dogs and cats running around Solid Anchor. The requirements were not stringent: All the denizens of the base needed were some sort of upper-body covering (either short- or long-sleeved); some sort of lower-body covering (ranging from cutoffs to dungarees); and some sort of head covering with branch of service and insignia of rank, so that people could tell whom (and what) everyone was authorized to be.

After that, Tief and Carter imposed a staff organization: N-1 (Personnel); N-2 (Intelligence); N-3 (Operations and Plans); and N-4 (Logistics). For anyone wishing to cross the Cua Lon River, it was no longer necessary to track down the lance corporal who happened to have the keys. Instead, you went to the N-4, who would provide boat, boatswain's mate, *and* keys, guaranteed to get you across the river, because that's what boatswain's mates are supposed to do, among other things.

Next, they fired the N-2. This earnest young officer's thorough training in Naval Intelligence somehow had failed to equip him with the basics of common sense. So, like many others similarly afflicted, he gravitated toward style in lieu of substance. Each day, he carefully charted all Vietcong sightings that were reported in his area of operations. Then each evening, after supper, he would brief the commanding officer of Solid Anchor on recent developments in the vicinity. Then, after an appropriate waiting period for questions, he carefully wiped his briefing board clean of all the day's markings, leaving it in pristine form to record the next day's activities. Thus, by voiding the institutional memory of enemy activity each day, the N-2 had become an operational briefer, not an intelligence officer. His replacement, a USMC captain, began plotting enemy sightings on acetate map overlays, which he saved—then stacked on top of each other until he began to see patterns of enemy activity emerge. These became the objectives of future offensive operations. Tief finally was getting the enemy in his gunsights.

Now there was a need to crank up the operational tempo. One fiasco on the part of the SEALs clearly showed where the need for improvement began. The SEAL team had stumbled upon a Vietcong communications-electronics repair facility, including even television sets awaiting repair, in the jungle near Nam Can. But instead of radioing for help, the SEALs ran through the site firing wildly, then began screaming over the radio for their own extraction by helicopter. Once back at Solid Anchor, they cleaned up their gear, enjoyed a leisurely dinner, then gave their initial report of their day in the bush at the CO's after-dinner briefing. Tief and Carter leaped out of their seats and ordered a Vietnamese Marine rifle company to be flown in to secure the area, but it was too late. The Vietcong had carried off everything, even the television sets. From that point on, the SEALs were on thin ice with Tief.

As the enemy became more clearly defined, the remaining problem became one of getting at him. Ground operations were out of the question, in an area with a ten-foot tidal range. The U.S. and Vietnamese swift boats that ran up and down the Cua Lon River could not carry many troops, and there were not many other boats available. In any event, boats alone were not enough to challenge Vietcong control of the numerous waterways of the Ca Mau Peninsula.

Early on, however, Colonel Tief noticed that the province chief always seemed to have a half-dozen or more helicopters parked on his spacious lawn each morning. So he requested support from the chief and, surprisingly enough, it was granted. The chief didn't always have enough for them to do each day, and he was happy to see "his" helicopters put to good use. Besides, the security of Solid Anchor and the Cua Lon River region definitely was in his best interest. He also made some of his Regional Force militiamen available to support the offensive operations out of Solid Anchor.

Marsh Carter took up the complex task of coordinating the assets and capabilities of the wide array of units now at Solid Anchor's disposal. As the ground operations officer, working in the naval operations center, he might pull together U.S. and Vietnamese river craft; U.S. Army and Navy aircraft; naval gunfire ships; airborne observers, riding in the back seats of the Black Ponies' OV-10 Broncos; and the aggressive Seventh Battalion of Vietnamese Marines, which had replaced the relatively ineffective Sixth Battalion shortly before Tief and Carter arrived. The tempo of operations was high, keeping the pressure on enemy forces that were growing more confused and discouraged each day.

Areas that the Vietnamese Navy had feared to enter for years suddenly came under attack. Tief and Carter also conducted large-unit attacks into the Dam Soi Secret Zone, which never had been entered by allied forces up to that point. If Vietcong defenders tried to hold their ground instead of scattering into the swamps in retreat, they became particularly vulnerable to the Sea Wolves, the U.S. Navy helicopter gunships that performed to highest expectations. No longer a haven for the Vietcong, Nam Can village doubled in size as woodcutters and watermen returned to the area. Charcoal and shrimp, two of the region's major products, once again were being sent northward to city markets.

At the time he took command of Solid Anchor, Colonel Tief requested the services of a second Vietnamese Marine battalion to increase the range and scope of his operations without weakening the defense of the base. The Vietnamese Joint General Staff would hear none of it. Instead, they wanted the Seventh Marine Battalion returned to its proper role as part of the elite national reserve force, in which it could be deployed anywhere in the country on short notice (for reasons that would become clearer within a month or two). The Twenty-first ARVN Division was the controlling Vietnamese Army force in that region, and the Joint General Staff leaned on Major General Nghi, its commander, to replace the 700-man Marine battalion with one of his own. Nghi was in no hurry to comply, and more than a month passed before he sent a 250-man battalion, worn down from operating in the U Minh Forest, to replace the Marines.

General Nghi had some reservations about placing one of his units under command of an American, and a Marine, at that. So he negotiated a curious command-relationships agreement with The Admiral, still serving as the senior U.S. naval officer in the Delta. Colonel Tief would have operational control of the battalion, but "supervision" would remain with General Nghi. This arrangement meant that, in the midst of battle, the battalion commander could refuse any of Tief's orders and appeal directly to Nghi. This placed Tief in the untenable position of being unable to rely on his principal ground-combat unit if the going got really sticky. Tief reported this matter both verbally and by message to the three-star commander of all U.S. naval forces in Vietnam.

The battalion from the Twenty-first ARVN Division performed well in its first two operations under Tief's operational control, without resorting to the "supervision" escape clause, but a back-door whispering campaign already was under way once again. This time, an individual, instead of the Vietnamese Marines in general, was the target, as Nghi's chief of staff falsely accused Colonel Tief of "disrespect." As in past episodes, the complaint did not move up the chain from commander to commander. It went from staff officer to staff officer until it reached the *deputy* commander of the U.S. Military Assistance Command, Vietnam, who passed it along to the senior Navy three-star with a request for Tief's relief. The request was promptly granted, without benefit of a formal or informal investigation or even a "What the hell's going on down there?" message or call.

Returning to Saigon, Colonel Tief encountered a distraught Vietnamese Marine commandant:

"What happened?" cried General Khang. "I tell you not to go down there. I tell you what those bastards do to you. I know those people say bad things about you."

For a Marine Corps officer, being summarily relieved of command in wartime is a career-stopper. Tief responded to this aberration with alacrity and vigor, setting the record straight in most forceful terms. The three-star admiral could not undo the relief action, and the cooperation of the

Twenty-first ARVN Division was essential for anything to keep happening at Solid Anchor, but he covered Colonel Tief with glory on his next report of fitness. This no doubt helped get Tief promoted to brigadier general but only on his second go-around—always an exceedingly long shot.

After Tief and Carter departed, Solid Anchor's utility as a base for offensive operations dropped off sharply, and the interim U.S. Navy base commander turned the whole bucket of worms over to the Vietnamese Navy two months later.

Someday, if and when all the records become available, it would be interesting to look for the real reasons that General Nghi had to get Colonel Tief out of there. It would not have been terribly unusual for an understanding—and perhaps a delicate balance of forces—to exist among the Vietnamese Navy, the Twenty-first ARVN Division, the province chief, and the Vietcong with regard to the division of spoils in this resource-rich area. If this indeed were the case, then Tief would have been a major fly in everyone's ointment, making such a balancing act impossible.

Someday, perhaps we will know. Stranger things have happened in Vietnam.

Chapter 10

Back in Saigon, the co-vans were locked in another struggle, not exactly to the death, although a possibility existed of its going that far if we pushed things hard enough.

The subject was jeeps and the Saigon street cowboys who were adept at stealing them. These cowboys, a breed of cat far different from our trusted Marine batmen in the field, were a particularly athletic form of street thief, whose most spectacular stunts were variants of purse-snatching from a speeding motorbike. Stealing jeeps, on the other hand, was a much more lucrative pastime, because the payoff was much bigger, and the Saigon cowboys were good at it.

We could chain a jeep to a tree and chain the brake pedal tightly to the steering wheel, and the cowboys would defeat the padlocks on those chains in a matter of seconds. We could open the hood, remove the distributor cap, and walk away with the jeep thus immobilized, only to return to find an empty space and some chains on the ground where the jeep should have been. Evidently, the cowboys had a black-market supply source for jeep distributor caps.

To cope with the problem, the Vietnamese Marines put a policy into effect: All jeeps would be parked inside the Bo Tu Lenh compound, under guard every night. When jeeps had to be taken outside at night with Vietnamese drivers, there was not much to worry about. As in the case of Ha-si

Quan of the Fourth Battalion, these drivers also were trained bodyguards, accomplished in the martial arts. In time, their reputations preceded them, and only the most foolhardy would-be jeep stealers were willing to tangle with the VNMC drivers. But when a co-van had to take out a jeep after dark—to greet a late arrival at Tan Son Nhut airport, for example—the odds suddenly shifted back toward the Saigon cowboys.

On one such night, I lost my jeep. Earlier that day, I had received a letter from my wife saying that our younger daughter, still a few weeks shy of her third birthday, was suffering from an infection that had left canker sores inside her mouth that made eating and swallowing quite difficult. Worried, I arranged an early evening long-distance telephone call back to the States with the Saigon USO, to talk to my family in Norfolk. How could I possibly console, from half a world away, a little girl in constant pain? I was able to park directly in front of the USO building, in a well-lit area with a constant stream of U.S. servicemen coming and going. Despite my preoccupation with the phone call, I remembered to chain the jeep to a tree and do the internal chain work to immobilize it before I went inside. The call went through quickly, and after a brief preliminary discussion with my wife, my daughter's clear, cheerful voice came through the receiver: "Hi, Daddy—I gots canker sores!"

She might have been bragging about a new red wagon. Relief flooded in, and I forgot my rehearsed words of consolation. She was going to be okay. I can't even remember the rest of the conversation. I hung up and walked outside, still warmed by the unexpectedly happy telephone visit.

It was gone.

This time, they didn't even leave the chains behind.

Up to this point, I had considered the jeep thefts to be a relatively minor irritation and even, at times, a source of amusement, considering the elaborate measures taken to foil the thieves. Now it was getting personal. What is the saying? Ah, yes: "The most ardent conservative is a liberal who has just been mugged."

It got even more personal a day or two later at the Bo Tu Lenh. A Vietnamese Marine from the G-4 logistics section brought me a paper and asked me to sign it, "to clear the books." I couldn't read all the Vietnamese words, which went well beyond our conversational crash course at Quan-

tico. But the document looked funny, too legalistic to be a simple statement of loss. Hell, in a combat zone, missing and damaged gear was written off quickly all the time. I called for our G-3 interpreter and asked him
to read the document aloud, word by word.

When he got to the part that said, ". . . and Thieu-Ta MILLER agrees to
indemnify the total cost. . . ," I thanked the interpreter and retrieved
the document from him. After tearing it neatly in half and placing the
unsigned bottom on the top half, I asked the messenger to take the paper
directly back to the G-4 officer, with my compliments. I heard nothing
more from the G-4 about clearing the books.

But I was hooked by now. I had been roughed up, and I wanted revenge.
I wanted to find out where these stolen jeeps were going, stop the flow—
and punish somebody, if possible. At first glance, it appeared that fencing a
hot jeep, even in the flourishing Saigon black market, would be a risky
proposition in a town swarming with military types. And other potential
buyers, such as the Vietcong forces just outside of Saigon, had managed to
do well enough without jeeps up to this point. A sudden influx of jeeps was
not likely to bring them a decided tactical or strategic advantage. The cus-
tomers, then, had to exist elsewhere. There was one extremely logical
source left: the Koreans.

To be sure, the South Korean units were well trained and well dis-
ciplined—aggressive in the field to a fault. But I recalled comparing notes
with one of their U.S. advisors. After I had explained our "trusted friend"
co-van relationship, I half expected him to describe a similar setup for me.

I was in for a surprise.

"Naw—it's not like that at all," he said. "Almost every morning, my
counterpart is in my face, demanding something, until I either give in or
throw him out of the office." There was not much closeness there. The
Koreans tended to think of us mainly as one great big goody locker, their
main source of supply. Whenever they wore out or break a piece of gear—
anything from a cartridge belt to a howitzer—the treaties said that we were
supposed to replace it from U.S. stocks. And if it was not brand new or
close to it, they would raise all kinds of hell. I don't think they kept much
of their new gear in Vietnam. Every week, a Korean amphibious ship left
Saigon for Seoul probably loaded with our gear.

"With the Vietnamese peasants," the advisor continued, "the Korean troops are mean as snakes. When they move into an area, they sit down on it so hard that nobody—bad guys, or good guys, for that matter—can breathe." After a while, the Vietcong would get discouraged and move on to another operating area, which suited the Koreans just fine. They did not seem to care about winning the war—or even taking the fight to the enemy. They are in Vietnam to collect U.S. gear, while suffering as few casualties as possible. The word was that every time a Korean trooper dies—for whatever reason—his division commander had to write a personal letter to the president of South Korea. He had to explain the circumstances and hope like hell that he would not be relieved of command for failing to meet the zero-casualties standard. It was almost a joke."

While we talked, I remembered another horror story about the Koreans: One of the hard-top highways leading into Da Nang went through a shanty-town area called "Dogpatch" by the USMC personnel who operated in the vicinity. From time to time, especially during rainy periods when the roads were slick, speeding military vehicles sometimes would hit pedestrians trying to cross the road or children playing too close to it. Then, an all-too-familiar scene would unfold. The driver and his passengers would get out of the vehicle to give aid to the victim if possible. They soon would be surrounded by a crowd of onlookers, and in due course the grieving family of the injured or deceased would arrive. Then the village elders would arrive and start to demand reparations, and things would begin to take a definite turn toward the ugly. If he had not already called in, the driver then would get on the radio and call for help. In time—and sometimes just in time—military police would arrive, accompanied by a claims officer who carried enough cash to make payments on the spot. After the family and some of the elders had been paid off, the crowd would disperse and the military vehicle would be allowed to continue its journey. Just another day in Dogpatch.

On one such rainy day, a South Korean six-by-six truck was speeding down the road and hit a young boy, evidently killing him instantly. The truck rolled to a stop a short distance beyond the point of impact, but the driver did not get out. Right on schedule, the local crowd began to gather, surrounding the truck. Then the Korean assistant driver climbed down from the passenger seat and walked back to the rear of the truck. He pulled down the tailgate, climbed into the truck bed, and uncovered a machine gun that had been mounted there. With slow, deliberate movements, he fed a belt of ammunition into the machine gun and pulled the operating handle to the rear to load the first round. Then, with his finger on the trigger, he waited.

Before long, a village elder arrived and launched into the customary demand for reparations. The Korean driver, still behind the wheel, just smiled at him. Then he started the truck, put it into reverse, and backed it slowly over the child's body. Then he put the truck into low gear, pulled forward across the child once again, and drove away slowly through the stunned crowd, which parted magically—just as dramatically as the Red Sea ever parted for Moses—to let him through. The Koreans liked to do things their way, which required no help from military policemen or claims officers.

With these scenes in mind, another co-van and I decided to drive down to the Saigon docks, to see if we could spot any of our vehicles being loaded out for Seoul. Even if the Koreans tried to conceal their monkey business by painting the jeeps blue, we would be on to it. The trip went smoothly until we got within six blocks of the waterfront, where we encountered our first Korean sentry, as diligent and unmoving as we ever could hope any U.S. Marine sentry to be. We pointed to our tiger suits and grinned a lot, trying to establish ourselves as brothers-in-arms. Having no way to know that our tiger suits were made of cloth from South Korea, he was not impressed. After a while, it became evident that he didn't know any English—or any Vietnamese, for that matter. And the only Korean word we knew was kimchi, the name of a pungent dish made from cabbage, and as the standoff continued we realized that we were moving into deeper and deeper kimchi by the second.

The unsmiling sentry brought his weapon sharply to port arms and gestured with the rifle barrel for us to back away. If we failed to give ground, he definitely would have chambered a round and repositioned his rifle once again, this time to aim in on us.

At that point, a number of thoughts began to crowd into my head. We already knew that this sentry was somewhat inflexible—even more than somewhat. And we knew that the Koreans in Vietnam were as mean as snakes. So unless this particular sentry was one in a million, he would shoot us without hesitation or remorse and probably never would be punished for it. No one would have to write to the president of Korea to explain *our* deaths. The final thought that rolled in was that, at this stage of my life, I was prepared to risk life and limb for certain things, such as fellow Marines fighting alongside me, but not for a miserable jeep.

My fellow co-van was in total agreement. We began to back away, wishing the sentry the best of all possible days, until we could turn around and scoot out of there. It was quite clear that this trail would lead us to no healthy or even useful place. We just had to do a better job of hanging on to the jeeps we had.

Later in that fall, a long-time friend, Marine Lieutenant Colonel Roger Badeker, invited me to visit him and his family in Thailand. Roger was the assistant naval attaché at our embassy in Bangkok, on a three-year tour. Several "Scatback" flights went from Tan Son Nhut airfield to Bangkok and back each week, so I could line up a short visit. Roger, who had paid his dues with an earlier tour in Vietnam, now lived in a Bangkok suburb that could have been located just outside the back gate of Camp Pendleton, California. He had a ranch-style house with carport, paved streets, and bus service at a nearby corner to an American school for his two children. And this idyllic scene was just ninety minutes away from the sandbags and barbed wire in the once-beautiful streets of Saigon (to say nothing of some of the far nastier locales outside that city).

After Roger had conducted a quick walk-through at the U.S. Embassy, he took me on a waterborne tour of Bangkok Harbor. For me, it was a great sightseeing treat, but Roger was just doing his job, part of which was to keep tabs on all the foreign-flagged ships in port, especially those from the Soviet bloc nations. To my surprise, there were more than a few of these, and I began to wonder out loud if the communists were using Bangkok as a new transshipment point, trying to work around our closure of the Cambodian port of Sihanoukville. But Roger assured me that the bloc shipping, though heavy, was no heavier than usual.

After the boat tour, we were walking through the city a few blocks from the embassy when Roger pointed to an undistinguished-looking bar.

"Want to see some Soviet agents?"

"Why not?"

"Let's go in. This is a favorite KGB hangout."

And sure enough, there they were: about a half-dozen Soviets sitting at a round table with an American Marine, whom I had seen on the Scatback flight. He was a captain who had come to Bangkok to brief senior U.S. and Thai officials on some top-secret sensor equipment being used in Vietnam. Everyone was in civilian clothes, but the KGB agents evidently knew something about the new Marine, because they were laughing it up with him like long-lost buddies. We could not tell from the number of empty bottles and glasses at the table how long they had been at it. But they knew who Roger was, because they made no move to stop him or even slow him down when he marched up to the table and told the captain, in a low but intense voice: "Finish your drink quickly and leave here immediately. Say nothing more to anyone. Return directly to your quarters, and stay there. Report to me at the embassy at 0800 tomorrow."

With his dreams of a precious evening's liberty in Bangkok with his new-found buddies shot to pieces, the clueless captain complied. The next morning, he found out who everyone was.

The brief but pleasant stay with Roger and his family—once I got used to the sudden transformation from war to peace—convinced me that Bangkok would be an ideal spot for an R&R (rest-and-recreation) rendezvous with my wife the following spring. During my first tour in Vietnam, in 1965–66, there had been no such animal as R&R, at least not for the folks on the ragged edge of combat. In those early days of the Americanized version of the war, very few admirals, generals, or politicians foresaw a war that would stretch a decade into the future, becoming America's longest. Evidently, most of them failed to read or believe a prescient U.S. Army study, completed in 1948, which estimated that it would take five hundred thousand troops ten years to "pacify" Vietnam (not far off the mark, as things turned out). But among those of us who went into South Vietnam in the summer of 1965, there was talk for a while of wrapping things up and getting back home in time for Christmas—echoes of the Korean War in 1950. In both cases, however, reality had set in rather quickly.

Once the senior war planners realized that our commitment was likely to last longer than a single year, they had to make some basic personnel policy decisions. Units had been thrown into Vietnam as rapidly as we could move them, but in a war of this nature units could not be rotated in and out of combat on the precise schedule of peacetime deployments. Veteran warriors would leave and green replacements would enter the war zone as individuals, with tours of duty stabilized at one year. Next, the hierarchy set out to make that year in the war zone as comfortable as possible for the individuals unfortunate enough to be yanked out of their jobs and schools to be sent there. Soon, an unprecedented and burgeoning personnel support structure was establishing a ratio of ten rear-echelon types for every trigger puller. Of course, all these support folks needed some creature-comfort support of their own, so before long a significant part of the infrastructure was engaged in taking in each others' laundry, in a manner of speaking. And not much later, the notion of taking a week-long (or longer) time out in the middle of a combat tour—also unprecedented in our military history—had gained official approval, not only for the trigger pullers but for all the laundrymen, as well.

The availability of military or chartered jet airliners made possible the rapid transport of single personnel to Hawaii and exotic spots in the Far East, where they could get "screwed, blewed, and tattooed" in week-long endurance contests. Married personnel and those with Significant Others could obtain government-provided transport to a great variety of rendezvous sites, while covering their partners' travel expenses out of pocket. Either way, it was a good deal for all, administered by yet another wartime bureaucracy. And in due course, instead of a major aberration in our history of war fighting, R&R became a jealously guarded entitlement. I know. As I neared the halfway point in my own year-long tour, albeit the second one, I looked forward to my R&R in Bangkok, still months away, as much as any homesick eighteen-year-old draftee.

Back in Saigon, another bureaucratic problem was brewing. A few months earlier, Gen. Leonard F. Chapman, Jr., Commandant of the U.S.

Marine Corps, had made a visit to Vietnam, during which he called on Lt. Gen. Le Nguyen Khang, Commandant of the South Vietnamese Marine Corps. As they parted company, walking together toward a turning-up helicopter, General Khang asked General Chapman for some amtracs (tracked amphibious assault vehicles). Unprepared for this request, Chapman responded with the equivalent of a California Invitation (e.g., Hollywood's "Let's do lunch sometime"), to wit, "I don't see why we can't look into that." When this was first reported to the co-vans, we took it, at best, as a "Wait . . . out" signal or, at worst, a gentle brush-off. But the Vietnamese considered it to be a solemn commitment from a four-star general to a three-star general, not to be overturned with impunity. Perhaps all General Khang wanted was a couple of amtracs to parade through the streets of Saigon. But perhaps not—and the Vietnamese weren't saying.

To cover our six o'clock, I began to draw up a rough table of organization and table of equipment for a Vietnamese Marine amtrac battalion. Actually, it was more the equivalent of a U.S. Marine amtrac company, which was big enough to satisfy most of the needs of the Vietnamese Marines. The sheer size and cost of such an organization should have smothered the project in its infancy, to say nothing of a lack of tactical necessity or feasibility—an eight-knot amtrac cannot swim straight across a ten-knot river. But the Vietnamese persisted, and nobody at Headquarters, U.S. Marine Corps, would stand up and say, "This is ridiculous!" despite our earnest prompting.

The biggest problem with bringing in amtracs, however, was not shown on the tables of organization or equipment. It was maintenance. The nearest spot for depot-level maintenance was Taiwan, and did we really want that? And did the Chinese, who already had to fabricate many of the spare parts for their obsolescent LVTP5s, really want that? And even if both sides really wanted that, could they—and we—really afford it?

Nevertheless, the proposal for a Vietnamese amtrac "battalion" moved upward through the U.S. and Vietnamese chains of command, without objection or even words of caution. Staffers at Headquarters Marine Corps took great delight in telling us how much the proposal cracked them up, but none of them had the guts to say "No!" They just kept bucking the proposal up the chain of command while they professed to be laughing themselves silly. Finally the proposal reached the desk of General Lew Walt, the Assistant Commandant of the Marine Corps, who had been the I Corps commander and senior Marine in-country at the outset of the Americanized part of the Vietnam War. Surely, common sense would prevail at this level.

I could picture Big Lew Walt walking into the commandant's office with the proposal in hand, saying: "You didn't really promise General Khang an amtrac battalion, did you?"

And the commandant would reply, "Of course not! I just said we'd think about giving him a couple." And that would be the end of it.

But it never happened. The plan was approved, at the assistant commandant's level, for reasons still unknown.

It would take years to implement, of course. Implementation had barely begun when the United States started to pull the life-support plug on South Vietnam, violating its own earnest diplomatic and military assurances. I don't know how many LVTP5s got over there, possibly as a ploy to strengthen the Vietnamese Marines in the long run, through replacement in kind by the much more capable LVTP7s, which were just beginning to come off the production line. Today, there still may be a couple of the P5s resting on blocks in front of the Song Tang Officers' Club, with flowers growing in them, for all I know.

While the amtrac battalion proposal worked its way through the U.S. Marine Corps hierarchy in search of funding, it also needed approval in concept from the South Vietnamese Joint General Staff, in their own budget hearings. I helped my counterpart, Lieutenant Colonel Luong, in making the case. There was not a great amount of enthusiasm for the idea on the part of the ARVN officers, but if the U.S. Marines would fund it without cutting the ARVN's funds, there also was not a great amount of opposition. So the ho-hum hearings became a merry minuet of pro forma assertions and rebuttals, with the outcome actually known before the proceedings began.

During a welcome break in the tedious hearings, I remained at the table with Laughing Larry Luong. An ARVN colonel sitting next to Luong began a tirade—in Vietnamese, of course—about the American "shovel noses" and how they couldn't be trusted. Even though I was catching only three or four words out of every ten, I was getting the drift, so I decided to stay at the table, pretending to read things in my briefing folder.

The ARVN colonel continued his harangue and I continued to stare at my papers, until something must have tipped him off that I actually was following his conversation. Suddenly, he stopped and asked, "Hey—does he know what I'm saying?"

Laughing Larry did not laugh openly, but he barely suppressed a smug smile as he nodded gravely. That did it. The ARVN colonel had just lost face, hat, ass, and poncho. Sometimes, a minor triumph can keep you going in the midst of major adversity. Life can be sweet, at times.

But my appearances with Luong in the Joint General Staff headquarters were not all destined to be occasions of sweetness and light. In its sixteen-year history, the Vietnamese Marine Corps had been expanding steadily from a single-brigade force into a full division, with three infantry brigades and the types of combat support and combat service support units found in a U.S. Marine division, with the notable exception of amtracs and tanks. Increases in personnel had been taking place almost every year, as new infantry battalions and supporting units were placed in commission, then folded into ongoing operations in the field.

For their part, the co-vans would assist the Vietnamese Marine staff in preparing justifications for the increases. Once approval had been granted by the Joint General Staff, the co-vans then would update the appropriate tables of organization and tables of equipment to reflect the new realities. This tidy arrangement might have gone on forever but for the fact that growth costs money—beginning with the money needed to train, equip, and pay all the extra troops. And by the fall of 1970, nearly two years into a U.S. process of disengagement from South Vietnam, the money was beginning to dry up.

Colonel Tief and the co-vans saw this clearly, but we had a hard time warning our counterparts of hard times ahead, because they didn't want to hear the message. After many entreaties, we managed to convince the Vietnamese Marine staff to develop a Plan B, which would incorporate some internal reshuffling within current personnel ceilings, just in case the request for a strength increase might not be approved. The Vietnamese seemed to go along with our suggestion, but I never saw a copy of Plan B, which evidently had been filed away quickly in some inaccessible place. As the time for budget hearings approached, we continued to tell the Vietnamese that Plan A was a non-starter and we could not support it. This, of course, was not what they wanted to hear, so they didn't listen.

On the day Luong and I walked into the Joint General Staff headquarters for the budget sessions, I was feeling like a whore in church, about to bring a lot of high-minded individuals crashing down to reality. In retrospect, I should have felt like a saint in a whorehouse, presenting a clarion call for prudence and moderation. When his turn arrived, Luong got up and did a masterful job of briefing, as I had feared, Plan A. As he returned to his seat, he gave me a nervous smile and an I-was-only-following-orders look. The panelists from the Joint General Staff looked my way expectantly, for the pro forma endorsement from the advisory unit. After all was said and done, of course, it would be U.S. dollars that funded this requested personnel increase.

I got to my feet. It was time to end this charade.

"The Senior Marine Advisor does not support this request," I said.

It was the moment of truth, and for a moment, time was suspended. The anticipatory smiles on the faces of the Joint General Staff officers sagged into slack-jawed amazement, then hardened into tight-lipped frustration as the full import of my statement dawned on them: All of this had been a waste of time. Why had Luong made the detailed proposal, if he knew the Americans would not support it? Had the American thieu-ta double-crossed him? Or did he try to pressure the co-van into agreement by placing him in a difficult situation, which threatened a U.S. loss of face?

There was plenty of face being lost in that room at that moment, but none of it was mine. The staff officers were closing their books and preparing to leave. There would be no fall-back presentation of a Plan B, even if Luong had a copy with him. I glanced back at Luong and gave him my own I-was-only-following-orders look, but he didn't look back. He was busily shoving papers into his briefcase and didn't look as though he intended to walk out of the room arm-in-arm with me. But this brush-off was just a hint.

Back at the Bo Tu Lenh, Colonel Tief's attempts to mend some fences were getting nowhere. His calls to the commandant and assistant commandant of the Vietnamese Marines could not get through. Lieutenant General Khang was reported to be out of town, at his country estate, and would be incommunicado for four or five days, at least. Colonel Lan usually was not anyone to avoid unpleasant situations, but he was nowhere to be found, either. A Bamboo Curtain had come down.

After a few days, common sense began to return to the picture. By refusing to listen to their co-vans, General Khang and company had brought upon themselves a temporary setback; by keeping their heads stuck in a very dark place, they might make it permanent. If there were any doubts up to now, it was becoming quite clear that Uncle Sam's cash cow was beginning to go dry. The Vietnamese Marines would need all the help they could get from the co-vans. Within a week, things were back to normal; a bit later, work commenced on Plan B.

The expansion of the Vietnamese Marine Corps had reached a new plateau, and there was some catching up to do. Over the preceding year or so, the VNMC had added their final three infantry battalions and one artillery battalion, a brigade headquarters, an engineer company, and a division artillery headquarters. This brought the authorized end strength to more than thirteen thousand men, a goal that twelve recruiting teams scattered throughout South Vietnam was meeting by bringing in an average of more than seven hundred new enlistees per month.

All of these new people had to be housed and trained. Six new base camps were under construction, and eight of the older ones needed rehabilitation work. In addition, the Training Center at Thu Duc had to be expanded to handle the influx of recruits and to provide adequate housing for more than seven thousand Marines' families who required shelter. And construction of buildings was just the beginning. In effect, a new city was under construction, with a need for new or improved roads, drainage, and sewage systems, along with water supply, electrical, and plumbing installation. This was largely a self-help project spearheaded by the Vietnamese Marine engineers, with a great deal of support and guidance coming from the engineer co-van, the U.S. Navy's SeaBees, and engineering specialists provided by higher U.S. Marine headquarters.

Going beyond the mere sheltering of dependents, such necessary adjuncts of family life as schools, churches, community buildings, a hospital and maternity clinic, and a commissary and post exchange complex were needed. To carry things even further, the most affordable way for the Vietnamese Marines and their families to stock their commissary was to grow as much of their own food as possible. In addition to vegetable gardens, this meant farms for raising chickens, ducks, rabbits, fish, and swine.

In this regard, the Vietnamese ran into a streak of luck when Maj. Gene Harrison was assigned as the senior co-van at Thu Duc, following his stint as senior advisor to Brigade 258 during Operation Vu Ninh XII. In addition to having U.S. recruit-training experience, Gene also had been a farmer and a county agent in Florida before joining the Marine Corps, offering truly a unique combination of talent and experience. After taking a look at the pig farm and checking the production records, he concluded that the strain of swine the Vietnamese were breeding was poorly suited to the Southeast Asian climate. The survival rate was too low, and the pigs that did survive were underweight. Gene hitched a space-available plane ride to the Philippines, where he located a strain of swine that was flourishing in a similarly hot, humid environment. He brought back enough pigs to make a fresh start, and by the end of the next breeding cycle had begun to see a major payoff for his efforts. Gene had truly become the Mayor of Thu Duc

All of this activity in justifying expansion of the Vietnamese Marine Corps and then dealing with its many ramifications would have kept any advisory unit busy, if not swamped. But there also was a war on, and our primary mission was not to feather anyone's nest but to fight in that war. Even while base camps and dependents' facilities were being built, the Vietnamese Marines kept an average of 90 percent of their units in the field, in combat.

It was hard to keep this in mind while in Saigon, which, despite its ugly scars of sandbags and barbed wire, seemed remote from the war that still persisted in the surrounding countryside. Perhaps it was a time of equipoise, as the roller coaster paused at the top of the track before another sickening downward plunge. As the Americans lowered their presence and kept handing more and more of the reins back to the South Vietnamese, the feeling seemed to grow that the war was already won. After all, couldn't vehicles move from the Demilitarized Zone to the Delta without armed escorts? What better test than that? And fear of bomb and grenade attacks on hotels and restaurants frequented by Americans had seemed almost to vanish.

Saigon still had its occasional moments, however. One evening, the engineer co-van and another advisor went out to the Tan Son Nhut airport to greet a new arrival from Da Nang, an engineer officer loaned by the III Marine Amphibious Force to help with construction work at Thu Duc. The new officer arrived while the evening was still young, so the co-vans decided to show him some Saigon night life on their way back to the Splendid Hotel. A logical starting point was the Hoa Binh bar, packed with its usual standing-room-only crowd, including a lady of the evening from Australia whose street handle was "Big Red."

Not alone among women of her profession, Big Red had a somewhat excitable nature, especially so when fueled by alcohol. And even though the patrons of the Hoa Binh had seen Big Red explode before—usually in response to a perceived personal slight, say, an implication that her charms were not worth the asking price—no one was even slightly prepared for that evening's bravura performance. Evidently, a prospective customer had disparaged Big Red's charms in a particularly contemptuous way, provoking her to reach under her skirt and pull out a pistol of undetermined caliber that had been holstered on the inside of one of her ample thighs. With an outraged scream, Big Red began firing wildly about the room. It was amazing that none of the shots hit anyone, but one ricochet round caught a boot heel of the brand-new engineer, less than two hours after his arrival in Saigon.

The co-vans hustled him out of the Hoa Binh before the White Mice arrived to investigate and took him directly to the Splendid, where I recall him appearing a bit shaken by the evening's events. The next day, he was taken to Thu Duc, where he vowed to stay for the rest of his temporary duty. Big Red's normal rounds never carried her as far out of Saigon as Thu Duc.

Most evenings, parts of the real war still were visible in Saigon. From the various rooftop restaurants, diners could see occasional flashes of artillery fire on the horizon. But most of that was outgoing, called harassing-and-interdiction fire. It was fired at random on likely enemy night travel routes, hoping at best for a lucky hit or at worst to make the enemy nervous and less likely to travel freely under cover of darkness. As things usually worked out, both of these hopes fell into the category of wishful thinking.

In contrast to that darkness, broken by sporadic flashes that blossomed along most of the horizon like distant pulses of heat lightning, the defensive sector manned by the Thai contingent was bathed in nearly constant light. Almost without letup, strings of flares would pop high in the sky, then begin their slow, flickering descent, only to be replaced with more high-poppers once they neared the ground and flamed out.

Defending a position from ground attack at night can be a spooky undertaking for the untrained and uninitiated, but the experienced foot soldier knows that anyone who stays down in his foxhole at night has a natural advantage over anyone who must move about, unprotected by terrain, in the dark. The Thais just wanted to take advantage of this, while removing the spookiness factor. This was an expensive proposition, to be sure. But as long as the Americans ultimately would foot the bill, why should the Thais incur any additional risk, just to save the Americans a few dollars here and there?

Just as life would begin to settle into an almost-peacetime routine, reality inevitably would intrude. Returning to the Splendid Hotel one gray fall afternoon, I heard the announcement, over the Armed Forces Radio and Television Service, of the death of Lt. Col. Bill Leftwich, U.S. Marine Corps. Operating in the Da Nang tactical area of responsibility while commanding the 3d Reconnaissance Battalion, he died while supervising the extraction of a beleaguered reconnaissance team, after his helicopter was hit by ground fire. I had never served with him or even met him, but I felt a sense of personal loss. His formidable service reputation preceded him wherever he went in the Corps. He had been a standout at the U.S. Naval Academy, and had received the Navy Cross for heroism during an earlier tour as a co-van, back in the days when only a relatively few U.S. Marines had set foot in Vietnam.

Early in 1965, the Vietnamese Marines, responding to orders from the Joint General Staff, formed a two-battalion task force to augment ARVN forces in Binh Dinh Province. Then-Major Bill Leftwich was the senior task force advisor. On its way to relieve the besieged district town of Hai An, the task force learned that one VC battalion had entered the town and another had taken up positions on the outskirts, to ambush any relief column. After a ten-mile forced march, the Marine task force left the main road into Hai An and attacked the VC battalion on the flank of its ambush position.

Major Leftwich, anticipating a need for close air support, had made arrangements before the task force started out. Once contact was made with the VC, he moved forward to the lead rifle companies to control air strikes. The task force attacked until dusk, when the VC broke contact and retreated into the settling darkness, leaving sixty-three killed in action. The Marines suffered only four killed and eleven wounded, but this included two co-vans: Major Leftwich was wounded and evacuated; his assistant, 1st Lt. Dempsey Williams, was killed in action. Bill Leftwich returned to duty after seventeen days in the hospital. Sometime later, he received the Navy Cross for his heroism at Hai An. Lieutenant Williams received a posthumous award of the Silver Star Medal.

As he wrapped up his advisory tour, Major Leftwich articulated the co-van philosophy in his after-tour report:

So much has been written about the advisory business that I felt some sort of mystic aura has grown up around the much overworked subject of "rapport." My modest experience with the Vietnamese, and that of many others, is that they generally recognize, admire, and respond to the same qualities that we—or any nationality—do. There are peculiar customs to be sure, but these are insignificant beside those characteristics that transcend all boundaries of language and nationality. The officer who is knowledge-able in his trade, unafraid of work, well-mannered, and possessed of a sense of humor will succeed here as he does everywhere else. . . . A single American is obviously casting his lot with his counterparts and is generally accepted on this basis, unless he isolates himself by his own misactions.

Bill Leftwich was only five years my senior, but he already was widely touted to be a future Commandant of the Marine Corps, a fighting service that usually casts a jaundiced eye upon anyone who might receive such acclaim so early in the game. What a miserable waste it was to lose him, especially after most of the action in I Corps was over and most of the U.S. Marines there were on the way home, and with Saigon behaving as though the war was practically won, whether or not it actually was.

My frequent trips to the MACV headquarters cave and Joint General Staff headquarters, probing for new information, did little to dispel this illusion. In the months since the Cambodian incursion, the Vietnamese Marines had shifted their center of gravity back into Vietnam, with two brigades—147 and 258, each with three infantry battalions and one artillery battalion—operating in the northernmost Military Region I. These were largely reconnaissance-in-force operations, with little in the way of heavy contact with the enemy. Brigade 369, also composed of three infantry battalions and an artillery battalion after the Ninth Marine Battalion completed its shakedown training and entered active service in September, remained in Cambodia. North Vietnamese Army and Vietcong forces generally had withdrawn westward, rather than fight to hold their base camps and supply areas along the Vietnamese-Cambodian border or their port facilities at Sihanoukville. Nevertheless, Brigade 369 had taken part in the fight to open Highway No. 4 between Phnom Penh and Sihanoukville and was keeping Highway No. 1 open between the Neak Luong ferry site and the town of Kampong Trabok. It also was taking part in Operation Tran Hung Dao XVI, designed to ensure safe passage of shipping up the Mekong River to Phnom Penh, where it had prevailed in clashes with the 493d Vietcong Battalion.

The absence of heavy contact anywhere was somewhat unsettling, carrying with it the underlying feeling of the lull before the storm. Were the enemy forces still licking their wounds from the Cambodian incursion a few months earlier (possible in the south; unlikely in the north)? Or were they marshaling their forces for a big push somewhere (unlikely in the south; quite possible in the north)?

From many trips to the G-2 section at MACV, I had come to appreciate the ghostly speed with which the North Vietnamese Army could create new multi-division fronts out of thin air, just days after the appearance of two men with binoculars—the prospective front commander and his operations officer—on a hillside overlooking the intended area of operations. But if anyone knew anything more, no one was saying. My fact-and-rumor-finding visits to my contacts on the Joint General Staff were bringing similar disappointing results. There was a feeling that something might be up, but no one was talking about it yet.

My visits to our units in the field also had these undertones of unreality, of time in suspension. Since relatively few large U.S. aircraft were flying at this time, when the Americans were pulling out as fast as possible, the aircraft most available for these trips were C-10 executive aircraft that could carry passengers north to Da Nang, Phu Bai, or sometimes Dong Ha, for further helicopter or ground transport to the units on the line. These once-busy airfields now carried only a fraction of their usual traffic, and were beginning to look a bit ragged around the edges, a sure-fire indicator of austere manning and diminished use. Compared to the pace of military activity in Cambodia and around Solid Anchor, the operational tempo in Military Region I was at a near-standstill. The reconnaissance-in-force operations were not turning up much in the way of large enemy formations, and this was an unusual state of affairs.

Even our "parent" headquarters of the Commander, Naval Forces Vietnam, was being distracted from time to time by matters outside the war zone. Within a few months of his leaving that headquarters earlier in 1970, Adm. Elmo Zumwalt was making his presence felt around his old command post again. In his new incarnation as Chief of Naval Operations, he had begun signing out a series of Navy-wide messages—soon to be known as "Z-grams"—that spelled out a series of bold new personnel policies, designed to challenge the status quo within a Navy that was moving into an uncertain future. These messages created both joy and consternation, the latter of which seemed to rise geometrically with the rank of the readers.

Against this backdrop, a couple of co-vans decided to rattle the cage of one of the senior staff officers in NavForV, a rather emotional commander, whose judgment could quickly become clouded when something raised his ire. He was, in other words, a "screamer."

One sunny morning, the commander arrived at his desk in the large staff officers' bull pen and found what purported to be newest Z-gram on top of his in-basket. It had all the correct message headings, date-time groups, and routing indicators, and it had been mimeographed, just like hard copy straight from the message center. The subject certainly seemed legitimate enough: a new policy that would end the Navy's recruiting difficulties, perhaps for all time. The policy focused on the rising birth rate among unwed Navy couples, or mothers, at any rate. The message spelled out a set of meticulously drawn instructions, complete with action agencies and reporting requirements. The women thus found to be in a family way would be transferred to regional prenatal battalions to await their blessed events. After birth and a mandatory recovery period, the infants were to be transferred to the Naval Orphans' Farm at Bainbridge, Maryland, where they would be raised by the Navy. At age eighteen, the orphan would join the U.S. Navy, thus permitting the mother or the father—depending upon the gender of the child—to retire or be discharged.

The message hooked the commander early on, or else he would have recognized it as a practical joke probably dating back to World War II, often played at the expense of long-suffering women Marines and others. But instead, his grip on the paper tightened and his head snapped back involuntarily as each new offensive phrase ("prenatal battalions," "Naval Orphans' Farm") came into view. His face turned bright red and his breathing grew labored, while just around the corner the co-vans got red in the face trying not to breathe or laugh out loud too soon.

Finally, the distraught commander reached the end and looked wildly around the room with mounting fury. Then he slammed the bogus Z-gram down on his desk and screamed—to no one in particular—as his fellow workers bent to their tasks: "By God—this time, he's gone too far!"

The hired help at the Splendid Hotel was beginning to take things more casually, as well. As I filled my pack for a trip to the field one day, the *mama-san* who cleaned the rooms on my floor pointed at the gear spread out on my bed, then covered her face as she began to giggle. She ran from the room and called a number of the other cleaning ladies over. Soon, the room was full of giggling females, and I couldn't figure out why. Their amusement seemed to center on a can of Wolf's Head brand chili I was taking along, to spice up any bowl of rice I might be invited to share. Finally, the *mama-san* started to say something:

"*Chó . . . chó . . .* ," she gasped, her face turning red from the giggling.

Chó is the Vietnamese word for "dog." The Wolf's Head label on the can looked a lot like a dog to anyone who had not seen a lot of wolves. The ladies must have thought that the American major had attended enough village banquets to develop a taste for dog meat and was carrying a can of this canine delicacy to the field.

It was true that dogs were seldom seen running around the villages, so the probability that I had ingested dog meat in one form or another, at one time or another, was rather high, although I never had knowingly eaten anything readily identifiable as a portion of a dog. I had no clear sense of how dog meat actually tasted, or of gradations of quality (as in white meat versus dark meat, working breeds versus house breeds, or mongrel versus pedigreed). So it was a bum rap, but the housemaids thought that the very idea was funny as hell.

Despite the disconcerting illusion in Saigon that peace was at hand—a growing body of evidence and rumors to the contrary—the 1970–71 holiday season was not much to write home about. Except for a few Americanized places like the big post exchange in the Cholon district, reminders of the commercial side of Christmas were relatively few. This was not as much of a relief as one might imagine, once accustomed to seeing Christmas advertising begin on All Saints Day. Over the years, it is possible to develop a taste for the truly tacky, and sudden withdrawal at Christmastime can create a deep longing for bubble lights, department-store Santas, and huge outdoor Christmas trees.

The spiritual side of Christmas did not seem to be much in evidence either, despite the high percentage of Roman Catholics among the Saigon elite. One shining exception was Handel's *Messiah*, performed at the downtown cathedral re-named, in a stunning bit of irony, for President John F. Kennedy, who had allowed the killing of President Diem to proceed just days before his own assassination in 1963. In any event, the cathedral was hardly more than a medium-sized church by Western standards, albeit a fine example of Gothic architecture.

On the evening of the Handel oratorio I arrived early to get a seat up front, ahead of the crowd. But the crowd never materialized, and I was able to maneuver my little wooden chair into the front row. All of the singers were Vietnamese, and they sang in English. The soloists were professional singers and handled their parts well, except for the basso, who could have used more power. The choir was well rehearsed and moved through the familiar early choruses in unremarkable fashion until they got to "For Unto Us A Child Is Born." As they neared the climax of that chorus, the tenor section took the high line so strongly on ". . . and His name shall be cal-led Wonderful . . . Counselor" that the glorious sound almost lifted me out of my seat. What a powerhouse! I sat there and marveled at the tenors for the rest of the concert. I never had heard any male singers drown out the sopranos before.

Christmas itself was a day to be gotten through. Some tried to sleep through most of it, after a strenuous Christmas Eve party in one of the co-van rooms at the Splendid. Armed Forces Radio had been playing a recording of *Messiah* that featured Australia's Joan Sutherland, a powerhouse in her own right as a soprano soloist. But once again, even the diva could not be heard above the din.

On New Year's Eve, I decided to get out of the Splendid Hotel, lest my own room become the venue for another co-van party, even more strenuous than the one on Christmas Eve. Another co-van knew of a large celebration on the outskirts of town. It turned out to be smoky, noisy, and crowded, with quite a few American civilians on hand. I took an instant dislike to one of them as soon as he opened his mouth and smiled his supercilious smile. The thing was, he had a really nice date, and for the life of me I couldn't see what she saw in him. After he overheard me questioning her about this, we had words. On this occasion, unlike the Fourth of July party, there was no U.S. Army captain to lead me away for a rooftop mortar shoot, but I found my own way to the building's rooftop terrace just before midnight. As some bells began to toll in the New Year, I looked toward the center of Saigon and saw a remarkable sight. The sky was ablaze with criss-crossing tracer rounds for a good ten to fifteen minutes. Since the ratio of tracers to regular ammunition in most ammo belts is one to five, the skies had to be filled with lead, all of which had to fall to earth somewhere and, to be hoped, not on too many somebodies. It was almost a victory display. Maybe the South Vietnamese really did think the war was practically won. Who was kidding whom?

After the fireworks display died down, I went back inside to the party. It was beginning to thin out, and my antagonist and his deluded girlfriend had evidently left. My American buddy, who was my ride home, also was gone, probably assuming that I had left when I retreated to the terrace. What a great way to start a new year. It was time to hit the bricks. I knew the general direction I had to travel, and it was going to be a long hike.

I went down to the street, and had not walked two blocks before two Americans drove by in a pickup truck and offered me a ride into town. I climbed into the truck bed and enjoyed a top-down drive through Saigon's nearly deserted streets. They dropped me off right in front of the Splendid.

Sometimes it is better to be lucky than rich.

The new year did not get very old before the close-hold combat operation became the worst-kept secret in town, buttressed by rumors abounding. Once the idea was out, everything fell into place. The logic should have been apparent from the outset.

The cross-border operation into Cambodia, begun in April 1970, had been a successful spoiling attack that allowed U.S. forces to disengage in the Mekong Delta, part of the massive withdrawal of Americans from Vietnam that had begun under President Richard Nixon. It also had the added advantage of drying up the seaborne supply route for North Vietnamese and Vietcong forces, which ran through the Cambodian port of Sihanoukville. This had a devastating effect on the communist forces in the southernmost of Vietnam's four military regions, making possible, among other things, the aggressive operations out of the Solid Anchor advanced tactical support base that were being driven by Col. Frank Tief and Capt. Marsh Carter.

In the meantime, the U.S. Navy's Market Time operations were interdicting other communist seaborne supply operations along the full length of the South Vietnamese coastline, and this hurt North Vietnamese and Vietcong forces deployed in all four military regions of South Vietnam.

This turn of events left only one lifeline for the North Vietnamese: the Ho Chi Minh Trail. The North Vietnamese knew that this network of highways, byways, trails, work-arounds, way stations, and supply caches had to remain intact, and also had to be expanded to make up for the losses in their seaborne supply. Late in 1970, MACV intelligence estimates began to show indications of a buildup for a major North Vietnamese offensive in the northernmost part of Military Region I, directed at protecting and improving the Ho Chi Minh Trail, as well as seizing the cities of Quang Tri and Hue. Aerial reconnaissance missions began to report increases in troop and vehicle movements down the Trail. This was reinforced by interrogation of agents and prisoners of war. In addition, the telltale "two men with binoculars" had made their appearance, and the MACV intelligence types noted the formation of a corps-level 70B Front, capable of controlling at least three divisions of infantry in an attack that appeared to be timed for the late-spring dry season in 1971.

So cutting the Gordian knot of intertwined routes known as the Ho Chi Minh Trail had become more than an attractive option: to disrupt North Vietnam's sole remaining supply lines to its units deployed in the South. It now was a compelling option: to mount a spoiling attack that would knock a major North Vietnamese offensive off track.

The precursor of the spoiling attack would be a massive assault from the air. The U.S. Seventh Air Force threw all available B-52s, backed by fixed-wing gunships, into a blistering air campaign aimed at turning the Ho Chi Minh Trail into the world's longest parking lot. The Air Force concentrated on choke points, where rugged terrain allowed the North Vietnamese to construct the fewest alternate routes. During the rainy fall months of 1970, the bombings and General Mud combined to virtually shut down the Ho Chi Minh Trail. But once the roads began to dry out, the traffic resumed with new vigor. Record numbers of trucks were destroyed from the air; but more and more supplies were getting through, indicating the total commitment of the North Vietnamese to their cause of "unifying" Vietnam under their rule. This evident dedication should have been a harbinger of what a cross-border operation into Laos would be facing. One story then in circulation spelled it out:

A chicken and a pig are walking down a road together. After a while, the chicken suggests that they stop and combine their resources for a ham-and-eggs breakfast. But the pig balks at the idea.

"A ham-and-eggs breakfast is an appealing idea until you think it through," says the pig. "You see, it might involve minor inconvenience for you—but for me, it would be a total commitment!"

In the amplifying fable:

A North Vietnamese cargo bearer has been given two 82-millimeter mortar rounds to carry down the Ho Chi Minh Trail into South Vietnam. For months, he suffers blazing heat; chilling monsoon rains, devastating air attacks, and swarms of malaria-bearing mosquitoes, while living on min-imal sleep and scarce rations. In time, he breaks through into a clearing in the South Vietnamese jungle, still carrying the 82-millimeter mortar rounds on his shoulders. A noncommissioned officer with a clipboard looks him over and says:

"Good. Set those two rounds down over there. And go back and get two more."

Sad, but true. This was how we sensed the determination of our foes, as we began to plan for a ground operation into Laos. And this sensing of their determination and total commitment proved to be not very far off the mark. The North Vietnamese had everything to lose in Military Region I, and they would not give way there. As soon as they began to sense that the air interdiction campaign was a precursor to a major land thrust across the Trail, they reinforced the 70B Front, building it into a force that included more than five infantry divisions, eight artillery regiments, six anti-aircraft regiments, and three tank battalions. The combination of rainy weather and air strikes during the fall of 1970 may have forced them to delay plans for their spring offensive deep into South Vietnam, but in the meantime they had amassed a formidable force, supported by relatively short supply lines into Laos, that was capable of defending the Ho Chi Minh Trail with many more troops—at least sixty thousand—than they could have sent into the South.

Preparing to attack the 70B Front was the strongest aggregation South Vietnam could muster, under I Corps commander Lt. Gen. Hoang Xuan

Lam. In addition to the First Infantry Division—the ARVN's biggest and best—General Lam had been given command of virtually the entire National Reserve Force: the Marine Division, the Airborne Division, and a Ranger group. Relatively lightly equipped, enabling rapid movement to trouble spots anywhere in South Vietnam and Cambodia, the elite Reserve Force would be bolstered by a First Armored Brigade task force, adding much-needed heft for the ground thrust into Laos.

The Nixon administration wanted to provide maximum U.S. support for this operation, but it was hamstrung by the Cooper-Church Amendment to the Defense Appropriations Act then in effect. The amendment denied funding for any U.S. ground forces operating outside the borders of South Vietnam. But Cooper-Church did not preclude air support over Laos or artillery support into Laos, if fired from the South Vietnamese side of the border. So fixed-wing air support (to include the B-52s, shifted from deep interdiction to tactical air support missions) directed by the Seventh Air Force and helicopter support from the U.S. Army's 101st Airborne (Airmobile) Division could be brought into the fight. In addition, the long-range guns of the U.S. Army's First Brigade of the Fifth Mechanized Division—sixteen 175-mm guns, eight 8-inch howitzers, and eighteen 155-mm howitzers—were emplaced as close to the border as feasible.

Sensing a real threat to the Ho Chi Minh Trail, and thus to their ultimate goal, the North Vietnamese had assembled their most formidable combined-arms force ever. For their part, recognizing that they had a major opportunity, for the first time in years, to halt the North Vietnamese infiltration into the South, the South Vietnamese were matching the Northerners in kind.

The biggest fight of South Vietnam's relatively short lifetime soon would be on.

As originally conceived in Washington and modified in Saigon, Lam Son 719 was to be a four-phase operation of roughly three months' duration. The ultimate objective was the Laotian town of Tchepone, in the middle of the North Vietnamese Army's Base Area 604, from which the South Vietnamese attacking force could presumably turn either northward or southward along the Ho Chi Minh Trail, ripping up the roads and support infrastructure and greatly slowing, if not stopping entirely, North Vietnamese efforts to supply and reinforce its units in the South. Taking Tchepone also would have the added benefit of preventing the North Vietnamese from applying pressure to U.S. units withdrawing from Military Region I, a goal largely attained in the Mekong Delta through the 1970 incursion into Cambodia. The informal word we co-vans got through Vietnamese sources was that Cambodia had been President Thieu's operation; the thrust into Laos would be backed primarily by Vice President Nguyen Cao Ky. Certainly, Thieu gave initial approval to the operational concept and had made an early visit to I Corps headquarters at Dong Ha. But Thieu's influence may well have contributed to early delays and a premature termination of the operation, once Tchepone barely had been reached. On the other hand, Ky and his wife, accompanied by their good friend Marine Commandant Khang, would go out as far as the Khe Sanh forward headquarters, during the thick of the fighting, to show support from Saigon.

The detailed plan was developed by a combined team from I Corps and the U.S. XXIV Corps, commanded by Lt. Gen. J. W. "Jock" Sutherland, U.S. Army, which would provide helicopter and artillery support from its bases in South Vietnam. Phase I would begin in January; South Vietnamese Army armor and mechanized forces would move to reopen Route 9 in South Vietnam. They would clear the route from the U.S. Marines' old Fire Support Base Vandergrift in Leatherneck Square, roughly twenty kilometers to the east, through the Khe Sanh combat base to the Laotian border. Early in February, South Vietnamese forces would kick off Phase II by crossing the Laotian border with an axis of advance along Route 9, and Lam Son 719 would be officially under way. Two brigades of the Vietnamese Marine Division would cross the border later in Phase II; one brigade would remain in South Vietnam with the mission of I Corps reserve. Phase III would encompass an orderly withdrawal of South Vietnamese forces from Laos, once they had disrupted or even shut down the Ho Chi Minh Trail. Phase IV would see the redeployment of South Vietnamese forces back to their home bases or to other operating areas within Vietnam.

Late in January, as the Route 9 reopening progressed, Col. Frank Tief

South Vietnamese Vice President Nguyen Cao Ky (in black air vice marshal's uniform), accompanied by his wife, Col. Bui The Lan (dark glasses), and Lt. Gen. Le Nguyen Khang, tours the Marine Division's command post during Operation Lam Son 719. The operation was widely thought to be Ky's special project.

and Capt. Marsh Carter returned from Solid Anchor, after its abrupt turn-over back to the Navy. Tief was seething, because of both the injustice of the charges lodged against him and the failure of the Commander, Naval Forces Vietnam, to investigate them. I accompanied Colonel Tief to the headquarters of ComNavForV, to hear him brief the three-star admiral in command on what really had happened at Solid Anchor. Tief's comments were succinct, forceful, and, above all, true; the admiral took them on board. Despite the unsatisfactory wrap-up of Solid Anchor, it was good to be rid of that albatross. We had much bigger problems up north.

As February began, Brigade 147, having re-formed after its stand down, was deployed to Quang Tri City by U.S. Air Force C-130 transports. A week later, the brigade moved in a truck convoy to Khe Sanh. Both Brigade 147 and Brigade 258, which was already operating southwest of Quang Tri City, reverted to the operational control of the Commanding General,

I Corps. The handwriting on the wall was clear: As soon as Brigade 369 could be pulled back from Cambodia, all three Marine brigades would be operating up north; for the first time, a Marine Division headquarters would be required in the field.

Lieutenant General Khang, the VNMC commandant, was senior to the I Corps Commander, Lieutenant General Lam, and on rather poor terms with him, to boot. So Col. Bui The Lan, the assistant commandant, was designated as the division commander, normally a two-star general's assignment. (In time, but not before the end of Lam Son 719, Colonel Lan would receive a promotion to brigadier general.) Lan's first order of business was to organize a field command group from the Bo Tu Lenh headquarters personnel in Saigon. This was no small task: establishing from scratch a mobile, around-the-clock, command-and-control and logistics setup that could communicate effectively with three brigades accustomed to independent operations. The network would include, as well, I Corps headquarters at Dong Ha, a host of supporting agencies, and the Bo Tu Lenh in Saigon. In addition to the imposing physical challenge of putting the necessary staff/agencies and equipment in place, there was an educational and cultural challenge in moving into division-level operations, which we were beginning to see only dimly at the time.

As these preparations continued, the lead elements of Lieutenant General Lam's I Corps task force completed the opening of Route 9 in western South Vietnam, reopened the Khe Sanh combat base, and crossed into Laos, thus officially launching Lam Son 719. The main axis of advance would continue to be Route 9, all the way to Tchepone, more than fifty kilometers into Laos. The ARVN First Armored Brigade Task Force drew the assignment of opening the road, which became infinitely more difficult than the job had been in Vietnam. Narrow, twisting Route 9 itself was in much worse shape than anyone had anticipated. The road was largely unimproved, and erosion had caused some deep cuts that would take precious time to bridge. The Airborne Division and the Ranger Group would sweep north of Route 9, establishing a string of artillery fire bases that could guard the armored task force's right flank and support its advance along the road. The First ARVN Division would operate the same way south of Route 9. The Vietnamese Marine Division initially was designated as I Corps reserve. It would be the last to cross into Laos, when so ordered

Within two days, the South Vietnamese had advanced nearly twenty kilometers, and the armored column had linked up with an airborne battalion at A Luoi. Then, despite this promising start, the ARVN forces stopped in their tracks. After two more days of inactivity, it became apparent that they were not gearing up to move out again. Word from South Vietnamese military sources was that President Thieu, during a visit to I Corps headquarters, had become concerned about heavy casualties suffered by some Airborne and Ranger units and the difficulty in making Route 9 passable for heavier forces. U.S. officers argued in vain that such delay would only give the North Vietnamese more time to stiffen their defenses, and their fears began to prove well founded as the fighting got heavier all along Route 9. As the 70B Front forces began their counterattacks against the suddenly static ARVN positions, however, they became more vulnerable to air strikes by B-52 bombers and tactical aviation fighter-bombers delivering close air support.

Nevertheless, despite their heavy losses, the strength of the defenders still seemed to increase. It soon became apparent that the enemy was throwing all he had into this battle, leaving barely more than one division in national reserve. He had no choice. Losing control of the Ho Chi Minh Trail would strand his forces then operating in the South—a point apparently lost on the South Vietnamese leadership.

By the end of February, Marine Brigade 369 had returned from Cambodia and had begun preparing for a quick move up north. Our newly formed division command group boarded U.S. Air Force C-130 transport aircraft for a flight directly into Khe Sanh. I had ridden in passenger-configured C-130s before. They could hold a lot of U.S. military passengers who could forgo creature comforts for the loading efficiency of four rows of cloth-webbing bucket seats, a row down each side and two down the middle of the aircraft.

When flying Vietnamese troops around, however, the Air Force loadmasters used a different technique, which might well have been called the Saigon Squeeze. Gone were the bucket seats and other webbing, and even though an exact head count was impossible under the circumstances, the loading ratio must have been something like three Vietnamese for one American in terms of space required, with an occasional jeep—ours, in this case—loaded on for good measure. Since seats were out of the question, seat belts were out of the question, as well.

After checking to see that our jeep was tied down properly, I slid into the driver's seat. At least I had a wheel to hang onto during the takeoff and landing. And the Marines already packed into the plane probably could handle the suddenly shifting weight of three Vietnamese better than they could that of one monster American. As things turned out, the pilot had enough runway at Khe Sanh to taxi to a relatively leisurely stop, rather than the gut-wrenching assault landing his aircraft could make with the aid of reverse-pitch props. My airborne jeep ride was a lot less bumpy than the ground versions usually were.

Shortly after our arrival at Khe Sanh, co-vans from Brigade 258 arrived by jeep and truck from Quang Tri City, after a tedious, dusty trip of more than 50 kilometers over Route 1 and Route 9. But they were grinning, and it felt good to be getting everybody back together again, albeit out here in the boondocks instead of back in Saigon. The weather was sunny and pleasantly cool, as it had been five years earlier on my first trip to Khe Sanh. I quickly picked out familiar terrain features: Hills 880 and 881, which dominated our plateau from the north; the forbidding, rocky face of the Co Roc escarpment, which towered over us just across the Laotian border a few miles to the west; and the slashes of red clay all over the place, wherever new roads, truck parks, and helicopter landing pads had been gouged out of the earth.

There was one major difference: Back in 1966, my U.S. Marine battalion, supported by a six-gun artillery battery, had searched a ten-kilometer circle, staying within range of our supporting 105-mm howitzers, for two weeks, looking in vain for signs of recent North Vietnamese or even (as reported) Chinese activity. Frustrated, the Third Marine Division commander ordered our battalion to hike back to the sea, some forty kilometers distant. He was baiting a multi-battalion trap, but the enemy didn't fall for it. The enemy was there, though. Two months later, the biggest battle of the war broke out in that area. Subsequently, the red clay of Khe Sanh became the focus of worldwide attention during a much-ballyhooed siege in which the besiegers suffered many more casualties than the besieged, while the far deadlier fights in the surrounding hills went largely unreported. Then, after a siege-breaking ground operation, the combat base was abandoned again, until it was reopened for Lam Son 719 some three years later.

The contrast between either the pristine Khe Sanh of 1966 or the heavily sandbagged fortress of 1968 and the bustling Corps-level base of 1971 could not have been more vivid. By the time the multi-division force—the tooth—had begun its thrust into Laos, most of its support echelons—the tail—had pulled into Khe Sanh. Rows upon rows of weapons, ammunition, vehicles, supplies, and even aircraft were staged hub-to-hub, wherever available space would permit, to the point of wretched excess.

I looked at an adjacent hillside, in the shadow of Co Roc, where at least fifty helicopters had been shut down. They were just sitting there, as the though the enemy were a hundred miles away. Tents going up all over the place added to the carnival atmosphere. Everything was above the ground,

Before the NVA artillery moved within range, much of the Khe Sanh plateau was a handy hub-to-hub parking lot for helicopters and vehicles.

covered for protection from the elements only, not from enemy attack. Didn't these guys know there was a war on—a really hot one, just twenty kilometers away?

This sense of unreality was reinforced when Lieutenant Colonel Luong and I made our first helicopter trip back to I Corps headquarters at Dong Ha. In a low, whitewashed building that looked as though it might have been a schoolhouse at one time, we heard the I Corps staff briefing on the upcoming heliborne assault conducted by Marine Brigade 147 into Laos, to establish fire support base Delta, some twenty-five kilometers southwest of the intersection of Route 9 and the border. Then the I Corps commander, Lieutenant General Lam himself, got up to add his own commentary. As Lam ran his pudgy hands over the situation map where the scheme of maneuver was marked, Luong whispered:

"We call General Lam 'Old Bloody Hands.' Every time he puts his hands on a map, more [of our] Marines bleed and die."

I didn't know quite what to make of that at the time. Luong smiled when he said it, but a trace of bitterness in his voice made it clear that he was not joking. I knew that Generals Khang and Lam had a history of mutual distrust; Luong seemed to imply that Lam would take his various frustrations out on the Marine Division entrusted to his command. Preposterous? Time would tell.

The following day, Brigade 147, consisting of the Second, Fourth, and Seventh (infantry) Battalions and supported by the Second (artillery) Battalion, moved into Laos. Almost immediately they became immersed in nearly continuous contact with North Vietnamese units, throughout their area of operations. Meanwhile, Brigade 369 and the remainder of the division command post completed their airlift from Saigon directly into Khe Sanh. They were wrapping up a four-day effort that used nearly a hundred C-130 sorties to haul 2,500 troops, 12 howitzers, 225 vehicles, and 280,000 pounds of general cargo. For the first time, the Vietnamese Marines were in the field, and in contact with the enemy, as a full division.

Within two more days, Brigade 258, consisting of the First, Third, and Eighth (infantry) Battalions and supported by the Third (artillery) Battalion, had crossed into Laos, relieved an ARVN unit on fire support base Hotel, near Route 9, and commenced operations to the northeast of Bri-

Early in Operation Lam Son 719, Senior Marine Advisor Col. Frank Tief *(right)*, Brigade 147 Commander Col. Hoang Thich Thong, and two staff officers visit the U.S. 101st Airborne (Airmobile) Division's headquarters at Camp Eagle to discuss aviation support.

gade 147, where it encountered the enemy on a more sporadic basis. Meanwhile, Brigade 369, in its I Corps reserve role, conducted local security and reconnaissance operations up to five kilometers southwest of Khe Sanh, with only light enemy contact.

All the battalion and brigade co-vans had traveled to Khe Sanh with their units, but the Cooper-Church amendment kept them from crossing the border, with the added insult of requiring them to sign a statement that they understood. As a concession, however, the Marines were allowed to have one advisor airborne over our division sector at any given time, so we set out to make the most of that small dispensation. We rotated the battalion and brigade advisors in U.S. Army command-and-control configured UH-1 "Hueys," accompanied by experienced Vietnamese Marine officers, to provide a continuous daylight presence over our area of operations. This airborne coordination team helped link units on the ground with the division combat operations center, in which the co-vans maintained a twenty-four-hour watch to assist in coordinating artillery fires, air strikes, helicopter support, and the like.

Staying in the air over that part of Laos was risky business, owing to the formidable North Vietnamese air defenses, which included antiaircraft guns that were radar-controlled and capable of reaching up to ten thousand feet. These guns would take a heavy toll of U.S. Army helicopters from the 101st Airborne (Airmobile) Division before Lam Son 719 ended; it is nothing short of miraculous that no co-vans were shot down. The advisors who spent the most time in the air received Silver Star medals for gallantry and intrepidity in the face of the enemy. No one could deserve those awards more.

During its first week in Laos, Brigade 147 remained in continuous, sometimes heavy, contact. In repelling a ground attack supported by mortar fire, the Fourth Battalion—the outcasts from Vung Tau—accounted for 130 North Vietnamese killed in action, against losses of 6 Marines killed and 42 wounded. The NVA attack was broken when long-range 175-mm and 8-inch artillery fires from the U.S. Army's guns near the border were brought within two hundred meters of the Marines' positions. A day later, the Fourth Battalion found more than a hundred additional NVA bodies, killed by a B-52 bomber strike. These computer-guided "Arc Light" strikes, launched from the Marianas Islands thousands of miles away, overflew Vietnam at such high altitudes that their victims seldom heard them coming. Their first and last indications of danger would be the earth erupting all around them, creating craters that were thirty feet deep. Even those far enough away from the impact area to avoid direct injury or death would be subject to blast overpressures severe enough to rupture their eardrums and leave them emotional basket cases.

Two days after the Arc Light strike, the Second Battalion engaged two NVA rifle companies and accounted for 145 enemy killed, at a cost of 14 killed and 91 wounded. In both the Fourth and the Second Battalion fights, roughly 30 percent of the enemy casualties were attributed to close air support.

During the same period, Brigade 258 accounted for 118 enemy killed in a series of scattered contacts, while losing 7 killed and 33 wounded. Even

Brigade 369, in Corps reserve back inside Vietnam, accounted for 10 enemy killed at a cost of 1 wounded. The enemy was everywhere, and the Vietnamese Marines were doing much better than holding their own in their first encounter with forces whose military sophistication and weaponry closely matched theirs.

This performance was most encouraging, in light of the fact that, despite the interruption in mail service caused by our move north, I knew that my wife was making final preparations to catch a charter flight to Bangkok for our long-scheduled R&R rendezvous. We were long past the point of trip cancellation and refund. Even if I could get word to her that we were in the midst of the biggest operation in years—and the fact that our Vietnamese buddies weren't taking any rest-and-recreation time-outs—we would take a financial bath with nothing to show for it. Besides, R&R had to be scheduled so far in advance that it was impossible to anticipate the operational climate that would prevail when the magic time finally arrived. And what's more, how could anyone say that the outcome of this longest war in our history would be changed by my missing a few days of it? There would be plenty more of Lam Son 719 left when I got back to it. And finally, who could say that I was leaving the South Vietnamese unattended, with such an able replacement as Capt. Marsh Carter—the ramrod of Solid Anchor— waiting to fill in for me? I had just about talked myself out of a major guilt trip, but there was one other factor that locked in the trip to Bangkok: The wife of the Senior Marine Advisor also was booked on a charter flight into Bangkok. And if Colonel Tief were undergoing any similar paroxysm of self-doubt, he sure as hell wasn't going to parade it in front of me or any of his subordinates.

There was no need for any discussion. Together, we turned things over to Col. Pat McMillan, the Assistant Senior Marine Advisor, and Capt. Marsh Carter, then we went back to Saigon, packed up some civilian clothes, and put ourselves on the waiting list for a Scatback flight to Bangkok.

Chapter 12

Colonel Tief and I got to Bangkok well ahead of our wives so that we could make final hotel and recreation arrangements. Each of us had his own plan. My plan was to start out in the lap of luxury, at the Dusit Thani, one of Bangkok's premier hotels. Then, after a couple of high-rent days, we would downshift to a Japanese-owned-and-operated hotel that was clean and efficiently run but much more reasonable because it did not provide all the frills of the Dusit Thani. After a few days there, we would travel to the beach resort at Pattya, on the Gulf of Siam, where the U.S. military had invested in Special Services lodgings priced for folks on R&R, and wind up—or wind down, as the case might be—the reunion. So far, so good.

It was advisable for the husbands and Significant Others to arrive early, after short flights in the same time zone. Most of the wives were in no condition to cope with the strange and unexpected on their arrival in Bangkok, after flying most of a day, halfway around the world. The R&R folks at the Bangkok air terminal had realized this, over time, and devised a way to preclude the chaos that ensues when a planeload of travel-weary wives is disgorged into a room full of waiting husbands. They placed the men on a balcony that overlooked the main terminal floor, then set up a series of room dividers to channel the women into the terminal one by one as they debarked from the aircraft.

This arrangement made it easy for a waiting husband to identify his wife from above and call to her to stay put while he ran down a short flight of stairs into the main terminal. But it also made things difficult for most wives—weary, confused, and dazzled by their arrival in the Orient—to cope right off the bat. One by one, they stumbled into the main terminal like early Christians entering a coliseum for an encounter with the lions, blinking in the light, uncertain. Their hesitation inevitably created a temporary paralysis at the head of the column, causing things to clog up farther back in the chute. On the afternoon of my wife's arrival, this brought an agonized call for action from one of the wives or Significant Others, clearly a woman of the Southwestern persuasion: "*Move,* you heifers!"

The heifers started moving, and the pace of reunions, tearful or otherwise, began to accelerate.

My own wife had not survived the trip well. She was totally exhausted and jet-lagged to the maximum extent: twelve time zones crossed, with night and day reversed. We went to the Dusit Thani, where she crashed amidst the luxurious sheets in our top-dollar room. I went down to the hotel bar, where I encountered an old retired U.S. Navy veteran. Nice guy. We had a pleasant, nostalgic conversation, which we could just as well have had in Saigon . . . or Washington, D.C. or almost any barroom anywhere.

By the next day, we were ready to abandon the Dusit Thani and go out on the town. I had seen a notice about a jam session for all the city's jazz musicians, which seemed promising. It exceeded all expectations. The musicians came from all parts of the Pacific, from Australia to the Philippines to South Korea. Most of the jazzmen we heard at the jam had gigs in town, and we could make a list of where everyone was playing and check some of these places out. It was great. Wherever we went in town, we had friends on the bandstand. Having expressed early her preference for Duke Ellington's "Satin Doll," my wife even received a few bars of entrance music a couple of times.

Bangkok, free from the pressures of war and much more a hub of international commerce than Saigon, had a cosmopolitan flavor, with distinct Western overtones in many places. Most of the jazz places we visited were U.S.-style nightclubs. I had a feeling that the Thai restaurants we visited for traditional Thai food, music, and dancing really were designed for foreign tourists, because that's mostly who we saw there. Throughout the city, we saw billboards and posters advertising a movie called *Hornet's Nest,* starring Rock Hudson and a European actress named Sylva Koscina.

After a brief taste of Dusit Thani luxury, it was time to downshift to the more economical hotel I had picked. Suddenly, we were back in the Orient again, only this time it was Japan. We may have been the only Westerners in the place. For a Japanese traveler or tourist, the setup was appealing. The tour, including food, lodging, transportation, just about everything, could be completely paid for with Japanese yen in Tokyo. The travelers would fly to Bangkok on Japan Air Lines, be met at the airport and taken to their Japanese hotel by Japanese guides and drivers. Their sightseeing and recreation sorties, paid for in advance, would be conducted in almost a pure Japanese-language environment. Except for a few minor instances, there would be virtually no need to read, speak, or listen to anything in the Thai language or to change money and buy anything directly from the Thai economy. Except for taxes, utilities, and other local drain-offs, just about all the money would stay in Japan.

Certainly, the Japanese were not alone in their ability to create a cocoon-like existence for their citizens overseas. I knew of U.S. military families in both Europe and Asia who spent full three-year tours without ever setting foot outside their U.S. bases. But the Japanese seemed to be raising the practice to a new art form.

After a few days in and out of our Japanese cocoon we were ready to move on to Pattya. It was midday when we arrived to board our bus at a terminal that was located next door to a radio-television shop. A loudspeaker was blasting a live broadcast of a heavyweight title fight in Madison Square Garden, under way at about the same hour the previous evening in New York time. A blue-collar Philadelphia fighter named "Smokin' Joe" Frazier was going up against a former heavyweight champion who had been named Cassius Clay until he first won the title from the menacing Sonny Liston. I knew that he later became a Muslim, took the name of Muhammad Ali, and exempted himself from the military draft, declaring that he didn't have any quarrel with any "Vietcongs." To his credit, he stepped up like a man and took his punishment, which included his suspension from professional boxing during his most competitive years. But in my book

back then, he was an ignorant, arrogant celebrity darling, being manipu-
lated by powerful forces far beyond his understanding, and I was pulling
with all my might for Frazier to pin his ears back, in Ali's first comeback
fight after the suspension was lifted.

As we waited for the bus and the fight moved into its later rounds, the
crowd on the sidewalk outside the radio-television shop grew larger and
more excited, even though the broadcast was in English. Near the end, Frazier drove Ali back across the ring with a devastating combination of
punches and scored a knockdown; it might have been enough to give him
the judges' decision. At that moment, the bus arrived. I didn't learn of the
decision in Frazier's favor until we got to Pattya, but the knockdown got
our beach trip off to a terrific start.

Pattya, too, was great. It had a nice beach fringed with palm trees and
lined with recreational facilities, all reasonably priced for the troops' thin
wallets, in contrast to other popular resorts in Hawaii and elsewhere. Pattya must have been one of the best-kept secrets in the R&R system, because
it wasn't all that crowded and that made things even nicer.

Early on, we ran into a U.S. Army captain and his wife who were great
fun but who also qualified as the Couple from Hell, who loved living life on
the edge and liked to take others out there with them. On the first afternoon, the captain and I went sailing in the Gulf of Siam, on what
amounted to a surfboard with a mast. We sailed pretty well, except that
every time we tried to come about, we capsized. Righting the surfboard was
not all that hard, and we would resume sailing, a lot wetter and a little
smarter, but not smart enough to keep from getting dumped into the water
again the next time we tried to come about. After a while it actually got to
be fun, in its own weird little way.

The next morning, we and the Couple from Hell found ourselves at the
head of a very short line at the parasailing concession. It looked easy
enough, and I, a seasoned veteran of seven parachute descents from perfectly good airplanes, stepped forward boldly to strap in for the first ride.
Getting airborne was easy, too—just a few steps down the beach toward the
water as the tow boat started to pull away and the chute filled with air. At
an altitude of a couple hundred feet, all the noises of earth melted away
and there was only the slight hiss of wind rushing by. Such a state of

suspension lasts for only a minute during a training jump from a thousand feet or so. The fifteen-minute ride ended much too quickly, and I had just about decided that I would go back up again as the boat turned back toward the beach. The plan was for the boat to cut power gradually to put me into a gentle guide slope. When my feet hit the sand, all I would have to do was walk out of the harness. Simple enough.

But the man at the helm evidently was inexperienced, because he cut power too sharply, and I began to plunge like a rock. The parachute was about the size of a U.S. Army T-10, and just as difficult to maneuver in the air. I was beginning to think that the landing was going to be a hard one, when the helmsman looked back, saw that I was dropping too quickly, and put on more power, but far too much power. This corrected my near-vertical guide path, but the sudden pull on the tow line and change of descent angle took some of the air out of my chute and I was coming down faster than ever, pulled by a boat that seemed to be going faster and faster. By now, we were past our cleared-away landing area and moving over a populated part of the beach. Sunbathers were beginning to look up at Godzilla Descending, and the ones who figured that they might be in harm's way were beginning to scatter. Then my parachute sideswiped a palm tree and went into even more of a collapse. It wasn't exactly a streamer by now, but it seemed like one to me. I was low enough now to hear earth sounds again, and the first recognizable sound was the voice of the wife unit of the Couple from Hell. She was running down the beach, snapping a camera as she screamed:

"John! John! I just got a great shot of your ass!"

Then I hit the ground. But instead of simply walking out of the harness, I kind of skidded in sideways, bounced a couple of times, then slid to a stop in the sand. Thanks to its quick-release feature, I was out of the parachute in a flash and running for the water. The saltiness stung in a few places where I had been rubbed raw, but I stayed in long enough to wash away the sand, which felt as though it was embedded under three layers of skin, and to ensure that I hadn't broken any bones. Then I walked slowly up the beach to the parasailing concession. The line that had been forming behind me seemed to have drifted away, and the owner, who had already replaced the hapless helmsman, was strapping into harness an athletic-

looking young Thai man, telling anyone within earshot how easy everything was, in a vain attempt to drum up some more business.

That was enough excitement for anyone's R&R. For the rest of the time
in Pattya, I was content to limit myself to sunburning and slow dancing.

Back in Bangkok, we visited Roger and Gaye Badeker at home. Before dinner, Roger switched on the televised evening news. I hadn't thought about
Lam Son 719 in days, and there was no film footage available for this
broadcast, but the graphics on the screen brought me right back into grim
reality. The South Vietnamese offensive seemed to be bogging down; North
Vietnamese opposition in the area seemed to be on the rise; and the
weather kept closing in. We didn't talk about it at the table, but Lam Son
719 would hang around for the rest of the evening, as an uninvited and
unwelcome presence. Things were going to hell up there, and that was
where I needed to be—not sightseeing or trying to kill myself parasailing or
otherwise avoiding the stark central reality of my life at that time.

Later, the somber mood persisted as Colonel Tief and I put our wives on
the plane back to the States. We didn't envy them the long trip they faced;
they didn't envy us our destination. Was R&R really worth it, if it was
going to end like this?

As the big chartered passenger jet began to taxi out to the flight line, we
walked in silence to the military part of the terminal to find a Scatback
flight back to Saigon.

Chapter 13

As Lam Son 719 matured and the weather worsened, the Khe Sanh combat base underwent a major transformation. Long gone was the sunny, lush green plateau with its State Fair atmosphere of tents and huge parking lots. As the enemy's long-range guns moved closer and closer, Khe Sanh had moved underground, into heavily sandbagged bunkers. Instead of consisting of a series of slashes of red clay gouged out of the vegetation, the combat base had become a sea of reddish mud wherever freshly turned, poorly draining earth had been subjected to day after day of driving rain. Even when it was not actually raining, the standing water in the muddy roads' deep ruts reflected a gray, sullen sky, intensifying the gloom-and-doom atmosphere of the place.

Upon arriving at Khe Sanh to stand in for the Senior Marine Advisor, Col. Pat McMillan saw two immediate problems: First, the Vietnamese Marine Division staff had gone underground, but for some reason the co-vans had not. Second, Khe Sanh was populated by too many co-vans with not enough to do. They could not accompany their units into Laos, and having only one advisor airborne at any given time during daylight hours did not create enough gainful employment in itself for seven battalions' worth of them. McMillan solved the latter problem by dispatching the underemployed advisors to make liaison with all the supporting artillery units in the area. If possible, these co-vans were to move in with these artillery units to stay abreast of all their moves or redeployments.

The first problem, however, required a bit more thought and a large measure of tact.

The co-vans had become lost in the scramble to burrow deep into the ground. Having no construction materials or heavy earth-moving equipment of their own, they depended on the Vietnamese for assistance, and none had been forthcoming. Part of the problem was a shortage of equipment: bulldozers, backhoes, forklifts, graders, and even sledgehammers. Compounding the difficulty, the division headquarters commandant and the assistant chief of staff G-4 were working independently, with no coordination. The headquarters commandant was responsible for setting up and protecting the command post; the G-4 was responsible for providing all the logistical support required for that job. But in the confusion of establishing a division command post in the field for the first time, neither officer had a clear understanding of the scope of his authority or responsibilities. One of the first casualties of this lack of coordination was a realistic list of priorities, and the advisor bunkers were not on anyone's list of priorities.

During the early stages of Lam Son 719, the Khe Sanh plateau became a tent city as endless convoys brought in a host of supporting units and their gear.

There also had been excessive delay in bunkering the U.S. Army radio-
teletype team that provided a crucial communications link between the
Marine Division and I Corps headquarters. Further evidence of lapses in
coordination was presented every time the tactical barbed wire within the
headquarters area was installed, then taken down, then reinstalled somewhere else.

The problem of getting the co-vans dug in took on a new urgency after
the first night Colonel McMillan and Capt. Marsh Carter spent at Khe
Sanh, sharing a shelter half tent, above ground. At first light the next
morning, Marsh unzipped his sleeping bag and opened the valve on his
portable stove, in hopes of creating a warm environment for dressing.
Unfortunately, he nodded off for a few—a few too many—moments, and
when he awoke again and struck a match to light the stove he nearly blew
the both of them out of the tent. Later that morning, Colonel McMillan
went to the Vietnamese Marine Division commander and pointed out
that he was losing face with his own officers by not providing for their
safety. Colonel Lan produced a bulldozer that very afternoon.

With bulldozer in hand, construction of a co-van bunker could begin.
Overseeing the job was the Marine first lieutenant engineer who, on temporary loan to the Marine Advisory Unit, had run afoul of Big Red in the
Hoa Binh bar on his first night in Saigon. Because he was in the midst of
his construction work at Thu Duc when his parent unit left Vietnam, he
had been reassigned to the Marine Advisory Unit as a co-van. At Khe Sanh,
he promptly had a long trench dug out of the red clay, in which he
emplaced vertical timbers on both sides. Then he had a horizontal timber
placed across each pair of vertical timbers and stopping there. Some advisors on the scene raised the possibility of more strength if the horizontal
timbers stretched *beyond* the vertical ones, to be anchored in solid ground
on each side of the trench. But the statics-trained engineer dismissed these
concerns as unnecessary. He then proceeded to cover the timbers with a
few sheets of corrugated metal, then some earth, then a few thousand
sandbags. The result was a bunker that was unlikely to withstand a direct
hit of an 82-mm mortar round, to say nothing of the 122-mm rockets and
130-mm guns the NVA were bringing within range of the Khe Sanh com-

After experiencing monsoon rains and NVA artillery attacks, Khe Sanh assumed an entirely different look as many of the tents were replaced by fortified bunkers.

bat base. But at least the long, narrow bunker got the co-vans out of the miserable weather.

On the bunker's first night, it sagged about a foot eastward, thanks to the soggy ground and the tremendous weight of the sandbags, and put about 50 percent of the Marine Advisory Unit in danger of being buried, warm and dry, in a mass grave of our own creation, had any NVA artillery rounds landed nearby. Fortunately, their gunners did not come close enough before the co-vans had completed some necessary shoring of their bunker.

Lieutenant General Lam's original hopes for a rapid armored thrust along Route 9 into Tchepone, followed by extensive destruction of Ho Chi Minh Trail caches and facilities, had grown dimmer with each passing day. The armored and mechanized units remained stalled on a road that had become nearly impassable. Even if further advances were made, it was not clear that they could be supported logistically, because only tracked vehicles stood a chance of making headway. In the meantime, North Vietnamese reinforcements continued to pour into the 70B Front area until they outnumbered the South Vietnamese attackers by nearly two to one.

Marine Brigades 147 and 258 had gone into Laos to release First ARVN Division troops from the responsibility of defending fire support bases Delta and Hotel, so they could move farther westward to support a final push on Tchepone. The final drive would not be on the ground along Route 9; instead, it would be a helicopter lift of two ARVN battalions from Khe Sanh into a landing zone about four kilometers northeast of Tchepone, followed by a ground attack into whatever remained of that deserted, destroyed town near the center of the NVA's Base Area 604. It would be the largest heliborne assault of the war, using 276 Hueys, accompanied by helicopter gunships and fixed-wing escort aircraft, in a continuous flight stream. Most of the aircraft would make three round trips that day.

Earlier helicopter assaults into landing zones south of Route 9 had suffered significant aircraft losses, and the antiaircraft artillery arrayed in the vicinity of Tchepone was known to be formidable. Warned about this, Lieutenant General Lam made the correct call for once, setting up B-52 bombing runs to soften up the area before the assault. These devastating air strikes not only wiped out the antiaircraft batteries but also dislodged enough earth from nearby ridges to uncover large underground supply caches. The helicopter operation was virtually unopposed, with only one aircraft disabled, and that from mechanical failure. When the two infantry battalions entered the shattered town itself, they found little more than the bodies of North Vietnamese soldiers killed by the B-52 strikes. After two days in Tchepone, searching in vain for anything of military value, they withdrew to a nearby firebase.

Resisting U.S. pressure to commit yet another South Vietnamese division to the campaign and to remain in Laos for another month to complete the disruption of the Ho Chi Minh Trail, President Thieu concluded that the objectives of Lam Son 719 had been attained by the brief occupation of Tchepone. Accordingly, he authorized the withdrawal of South Vietnamese units from Laos to begin. After all, even another division would not swing the relative strength of forces in his favor, and he was already committed to

A CH-47 Chinook from the 101st Airborne (Airmobile) Division lifts a damaged UH-1E Huey from Laos back to Camp Eagle.

the hilt, with his remaining National Reserve consisting only of Marine Brigade 369 at Khe Sanh. The North Vietnamese actually seemed to be gaining strength, and just the task of disengaging would be difficult enough. Lieutenant General Lam, who had placed the operation on hold while awaiting such welcome news from Saigon, promptly ordered the commencement of Phase III of Operation Lam Son 719.

Lieutenant General Lam called a commanders' conference at his I Corps headquarters at Dong Ha, to brief his plan for the withdrawal of forces from Laos. Colonel McMillan, accompanying Colonel Lan, the Marine Division commander, to the meeting, was struck by how hard the U.S. Army advisors were trying to remain in the background—as inconspicuous as potted palms—distancing themselves from any facet of the I Corps plan they undoubtedly had helped to create.

The briefing revealed Old Bloody Hands at his worst. The plan had only one objective—to extract the South Vietnamese *Army* forces from Laos. It called for Marine Brigade 147 to remain on fire support base Delta and Brigade 258 to remain on fire support base Hotel until all South Vietnamese *Army* units had cleared the border. Assuming quite correctly that Brigade 147 would be under severe pressure if it tried to withdraw from Delta through Brigade 258 at fire support base Hotel, the plan called for Brigade 147 to move south and east away from Khe Sanh and reenter South Vietnam in the vicinity of the A Shau Valley, an NVA stronghold. Lieutenant General Lam made no mention of fire support, air support, or logistic support for Brigade 147.

It was sheer madness, but Lieutenant General Sutherland, whose XXIV Corps of the U.S. Army normally would have provided a great deal of the unmentioned support, remained silent. Perhaps sensing the futility of a direct protest in those surroundings, the Marine Division commander remained silent, as well. The briefing was over.

On the helicopter flight back to Khe Sanh, Colonel Lan kept his own counsel. But as Colonel McMillan read his mood, there could be no doubt that Lan had absolutely no intention of executing a plan that had been designed to lead to the destruction of a large part of his Marine Division.

Little did the South Vietnamese commanders realize just how difficult the task of breaking away from the North Vietnamese death grip would be.

A withdrawal under pressure is one of the most dangerous and potentially disastrous of all military operations. The mechanics are clear, but no matter how skillfully a commander may leapfrog his withdrawing units behind successive lines of defense, he must contend with a steadily shifting balance of combat power in the pursuing enemy's favor. Ultimately, the final tiny remnants of the retreating force (known euphemistically as "units left in contact") must hold off the enemy's full strength, focused solely on them, to cover their withdrawing brothers-in-arms. Only then may they begin to think about fighting their way through their own escape to a safe haven. As a rule of thumb, withdrawing units suffer disproportionately high casualties, and casualty counts can skyrocket—if untrained troops give way to panic and let an orderly withdrawal become a rout.

Overcoming their initial shock at seeing their Ho Chi Minh lifeline to the south threatened so severely, the North Vietnamese had acted quickly to blunt the South Vietnamese offensive. And all the attributes that had made them able defenders of the Trail—including their knowledge of the terrain and their ability to use the miserable weather to their advantage—

would apply in spades as they pursued the erstwhile invaders back across the border. They had also learned to use their tanks effectively, in terrain and under weather conditions that hardly favored massed-armor shock tactics. Instead, they used their tanks as mobile gun platforms, avoiding the chopped-up main roads that had bogged down the ARVN tanks and finding ways to move through jungle trails to appear where and when they were least expected.

After a while, their patterns of operation became familiar. They would ambush retreating units to stop them in their tracks, then encircle them to cut them off from all help and grind them to dust. Against the South Vietnamese fire support bases strung along each side of Route 9 like grapes on a vine, their tactics were essentially the same. The NVA first would encircle the base, to cut off any landward reinforcement or support. Then they would start to close in, digging spider-web trenches when necessary to protect themselves from direct fire aimed at them from the defensive perimeter.

This was a classic NVA technique, known variously as "bear hug" or "grab them by the belt." The object was to get so close to one's enemy that he would hesitate to call in fire support from artillery, naval guns, B-52s, or even close air support, for fear of hitting his own troops. At times, helicopter pilots flying resupply missions would report that NVA troops, lying on their backs under the tactical barbed wire surrounding the firebases, were directing small-arms fire straight up at them. Then, as soon as the weather closed in enough to shut down close air support from fixed-wing aircraft, the NVA would bring up the tanks and overrun the base. In this manner they moved methodically down the grapevine that was Route 9, plucking the ripe grapes otherwise known as fire support bases, one by one, and building up intense pressure on the final grapes: Marine Brigades 147 and 258, on firebases Delta and Hotel.

There had been a lot of action around fire support base Delta since the second week of March. Heavy attacks by 82-mm mortars and 122-mm rockets continued for nearly a week before 130-mm guns, brought within range by the NVA, were added to the mix. Delta was manned by the Marines' Second Artillery Battalion and Seventh Infantry Battalion. The Second and Fourth Infantry Battalions operated away from the base, attempting to keep the NVA from closing in, but with little success. The Northerners were everywhere. Despite repeated appeals to I Corps for artillery and aerial support, the Marines remained at the very bottom of the priority list. Several efforts to resupply the fire support bases by helicopter were delayed because all gunship escorts were committed farther west. Fortunately, Delta had been stocked initially with ten days' supply of food and ammunition, which helped to prolong its staying power after the aerial resupply problem went from extremely difficult to impossible.

It was now becoming more and more evident that Delta was being encircled. The NVA appeared to be grabbing the Vietnamese Marines by the belt, moving in close enough to the encircled units to keep the defenders from making effective use of artillery or air support. On 15 March, the Second Infantry Battalion, exhausted after twelve days' continuous engagement with NVA units, broke contact and traded places with the Sev-

Part of the hands-on work of the co-vans was hooking up external loads to heavy-lift helicopters.

enth Battalion, coming down from Delta. Even the appearance of a relatively fresh battalion did little to change the steadily deteriorating situation, however. By now, pockets of NVA troops were working their way into
defilade positions on the steep slopes of Delta, where they could bring fire
to bear on approaching resupply and evacuation helicopters without being
hit by direct small-arms fire or indirect mortar fire from the base.

On 17 March, in conjunction with a B-52 strike, a resupply mission to
Delta got through—but with great difficulty, because of extremely heavy
antiaircraft fire. Ten active antiaircraft positions were silenced by fixed-
wing tactical aviation and helicopter gunships, only to reappear later in
new locations.

On the following day, the Fourth and Seventh Battalions began to sweep
back toward Delta, and hopes ran high that they would be able to clear
away the NVA troops who were making the resupply efforts so difficult. But
once they neared the perimeter of the base they went into a defensive
stance, and there was no evidence that the brigade commander was telling
them to do anything else. The Marine Division staff was finding it too hard
to break the old habits of granting autonomy to brigade commanders, and
Colonel Thong of Brigade 147 was becoming a major problem. He did not
tell the division his scheme of maneuver, and the division was reluctant to
ask him for one or impose one upon him. He refused to clear artillery and
air strikes within one thousand meters of Delta, nominally because of the
positioning of his reconnaissance units, but more likely because of his distrust of the accuracy of the supporting arms. He knew, for example, that
the Marine Division artillery batteries had not registered and were not pro-
ficient at delivering high-angle defensive fire, a must in this rugged terrain.
Thong also knew that misdirected close air support had killed and wounded
some of his warriors in the preceding two weeks.

This spell of apparent "bunker-itis" lasted for two more days and two
unsuccessful attempts at aerial resupply, which were driven off by heavy
antiaircraft fire. If Brigade 147 did not act to clear the NVA away from the
Delta perimeter, the base certainly would have to be evacuated. Five of the
ten 105-mm howitzers on Delta already had been damaged by enemy fire,
and the indirect-fire attacks, bolstered by the arrival of NVA 130-mm
guns, were stepping up in intensity.

On 21 March, the NVA launched a heavy ground attack with two regiments—the 29th and the 803rd—preceded by mortar and tank gun fire.
Frustrated by Colonel Thong's reluctance to bring in close supporting fires,
Colonel Lan overrode his brigade commander and called in a 175-mm
artillery barrage to break up NVA forces massing for the attack. And,
according to a POW report later, one battalion maneuvering away from
the artillery fire moved into the impact area of a B-52 strike and lost more
than four hundred killed.

During the attack, Chinese-speaking technicians monitoring NVA
radio transmissions reported hearing instructions being passed in their
language, as well as references in Vietnamese to "Chinese advisors." Wom-
en's voices also were heard, issuing commands. One VNMC company
commander could not resist a verbal duel with one of the females, after
she chided the "Saigon puppets" for relying on U.S. equipment: "Oh yeah?
And I suppose the radio you are using was made in Hanoi. You people
don't even know how to cook a bowl of rice!"

During the day, seven UH-1 helicopters—unarmed "slicks"—flew to
Delta with some resupply items and attempted to conduct an evacuation
of the wounded. They got through, where the much bigger CH-47s could
not, but all were hit by ground fire and one was destroyed. The intensity of
fire in the landing zone kept them from taking out any more than twelve
wounded Marines.

As the attack continued, the Marine Division commander requested
permission for Brigade 147 to conduct a night withdrawal from Delta that
evening. Lieutenant General Lam disapproved the request, at the same
time repeating his demand that the remaining howitzers be evacuated
from the fire support base, despite the fact that the only helicopters big
enough to lift them, the CH-47s, had been unable to land on Delta for
three days. Since most other South Vietnamese units had left Laos by now,
fire support priorities were about to shift to the Marines.

More B-52 strikes, like the one that had smashed an enemy battalion that
very day, would be scheduled throughout the following day. But this
proved to be a mixed blessing, when Marine requests to synchronize the

strikes to best support attempts at resupply and evacuation of howitzers from Delta were summarily rejected by higher headquarters. We now had a very large tail wagging a relatively small dog, with massive air strikes scheduled on an arbitrary basis that failed to take the tactical situation into account.

The final indignity, however, came at that evening's briefing by Lieutenant General Lam, when he grandly told Colonel Lan that he and the Marines had been allocated two thousand rounds of 8-inch gunfire and five thousand rounds of 155-mm artillery for the next day's fighting. In fact, Lam had already displaced those guns to positions farther from the border, and none of them were in range to provide fire support to Delta, where all that firepower was needed desperately.

"Now the Marines will have to fight," said Lam, quite satisfied with himself. Old Bloody Hands finally had shown his true colors as a would-be destroyer of Vietnamese Marines.

The NVA resumed the attack the next morning, after a ten-hour lull. The new priority in air support helped the Marines hold their own for a while. Fixed-wing air strikes went in to suppress antiaircraft fire, and helicopter gunships worked to strip the defensive perimeter of enemy troops. After four hours of this landing zone preparation, a flight of "slicks" bearing supplies took off for Delta, but the mission was scrubbed en route when one of the helicopters was shot down well north of the fire support base. This final attempt to resupply Delta ended with an unsuccessful parachute drop. Two loads landed in the tactical wire; two landed outside the perimeter, to be recovered by NVA troops.

In time, the NVA troops penetrated part of the perimeter and began to consolidate its forces in the center of Delta. Marine defenders were ordered to pull back from the center, to make way for more close-air-support strikes that would be bringing napalm along. But the strike aircraft were diverted at the last minute for a "higher priority" mission. Whatever that priority was—it sealed the fate of Brigade 147.

It was early in the evening when the NVA brought up ten tanks, all equipped with flamethrowers, to begin their final push. The Vietnamese Marines held their ground for a while, stopping two tanks with their light antitank assault weapons. A third was knocked out when it rolled over an antitank mine. A fourth tank, south of the fire support base, appeared to have been hit by an air strike.

The other six tanks got through.

The division commander then ordered Brigade 147 to begin a withdrawal toward fire support base Hotel, north of the Co Roc highlands. Next, he ordered Brigade 258 to secure a landing zone and provide a safe area for the helicopter evacuation of Brigade 147. It would be a fighting withdrawal. Route 9 had been interdicted by the North Vietnamese, who now sat astride the withdrawal route with two base camps, nine tanks in blocking positions, and numerous infantry units deployed—set in ambush positions—in the stream beds that led away from Delta.

The Second and Fourth Battalions, together with the artillerymen and the brigade command group, began to pull back through blocking positions established by the Seventh Battalion. Maj. Pat Carlisle, monitoring his battalion's radio calls from Khe Sanh, had the gut-wrenching experience of hearing his counterpart's call sign drop off the air, as the Second Battalion commander, Maj. Nguyen Xuan Phuc, calmly broadcast: "This is Saigon, shutting down for a while. . . . Out."

For the first time, the co-vans at Khe Sanh had to face the possibility that a full brigade of Vietnamese Marines might not make it back. It would be an agonizingly long night.

But by the next morning, elements of Brigades 147 and 258 had linked up near fire support base Hotel, where the Third Battalion had secured a landing zone. Major Phuc, though suffering from wounds, had led the Second Battalion out on foot, as had the other two infantry battalion commanders. One battalion executive officer's bodyguard, armed only with three hand grenades and a .45 pistol with seven rounds, singlehandedly took out three NVA outposts and became the singular hero of the withdrawal. An impressive degree of unit integrity was maintained, even though a number of small units got cut off and would have to evade larger NVA forces for up to four days before escaping back into South Vietnam. Of 134 Marines listed as missing in action from Delta, all but 37 eventually made it back across the border.

The commander of the supporting U.S. Army aviation units had made a personal promise to Colonel McMillan that he would set up a continuous "daisy chain" of helicopters to pick up Brigade 147 and fly it back to the Khe Sanh combat base, once they had broken clear of the NVA forces that were surrounding them at fire support base Delta. As Brigade 147 fought its way back to the border, the Army helicopters began to pick up units and deliver them to Khe Sanh. As the lift continued after dark, under lights set up by the Marine engineers, it was heartbreaking for co-vans to watch these tough Marines and their tough commanders disembark from the helicopters with tears streaming down their faces, shocked by the loss of brothers-in-arms who had fought alongside them for as long as fifteen years.

Midway through this evacuation, the U.S. Army aviation commander called by radio to say that he was going to shut off the lift. Colonel McMillan promptly declared a combat emergency. The Army commander decided to continue the lift.

The sense of relief was palpable. Just try to understand how the British must have felt about the miracle of Dunkirk, as Brigade 147 was helilifted into Khe Sanh over the next twenty-four hours. The brigade had been handled roughly in Laos, with casualties of 271 killed and 598 wounded, more than 200 of whom were returned to duty almost immediately. Major Phuc's "Crazy Water Buffalo" Second Battalion had been hardest hit, with 110 killed, 227 wounded, and 14 missing in action. During the final two-day assault on Delta, the Marines lost 60 killed and 150 wounded, while killing an estimated 600 NVA soldiers. Another 400 enemy died in the B-52 strike on the first day of the attack on Delta.

During nearly a month in Laos, the Marine Division as a whole accounted for more than 2,000 NVA killed, at a cost of 335 dead, 768 wounded, and 37 missing. Estimates of enemy casualties were slow and spotty in coming, but some indicators emerged early to show that the NVA had been hurt badly. A North Vietnamese radio broadcast, monitored a few evenings after the return to Khe Sanh, congratulated the 29th and 803rd NVA Regiments on their "annihilation" of Brigade 147, and added, almost too casually, that they were returning to North Vietnam for a well-deserved rest. U.S. intelligence analysts later calculated that the NVA lost sixteen of the thirty-three maneuver battalions it had committed to the Lam Son 719 area of operations. These were not units that had suffered enough damage to be rendered ineffective; these units were *lost:* destroyed, dropped from the Order of Battle.

At the time of Brigade 147's return, however, it was far too early to compare casualties. The prevailing feeling was one of profound relief and concern for the condition of the Marines. Some of the co-vans who turned out to greet them saw fear in the eyes of many young troopers, reflecting the terrors of their fighting withdrawal from Delta. They didn't feel victorious; the NVA had kicked them off their fire support base and made them fear for their lives. But the ability of the human spirit to rebound is astounding. Within twenty-four hours, these same Marines were back in the hills with their units, covering the southern approaches into Khe Sanh. Wherever they were unable to replace missing gear, they improvised, even fashioning new backpacks from gunny sacks and communication wire.

It probably was just as well that the young Marines of Brigade 147 were not aware of an even more lethal threat they had recently faced. Shortly after the withdrawal from Delta began, the Marine Division command post was notified of a B-52 strike, inbound from Guam, scheduled less than two hours away. Planned with no knowledge of the tactical situation on the ground, in typical tail-wags-dog fashion, the strike would fall directly across the withdrawal route of Brigade 147.

Armed only with his working knowledge of the U.S. Air Force's command hierarchy, Capt. Marsh Carter worked his way by radio back to Seventh Air Force headquarters in Saigon, the lowest echelon that could abort the strike. It was more than a communications problem; he also had to overcome the wag-the-dog mind-set that automatically called for the endangered friendly troops to get out of the way. In this case, moving away from the strike area would require a force that was withdrawing under severe pressure, out of radio contact, to reverse course and drive at least one kilometer through its attackers back into Laos, away from all friendly support, all within two hours. With grim persistence, Marsh succeeded in overcoming each layer of bureaucratic inertia with the sheer logic of his position.

Perhaps his toughest moments came in trying to dislodge a do-less U.S.

Army XXIV Corps duty officer, who was moved to action only after Marsh and this voice on his radio agreed to exchange "I know who you are" service numbers, before he granted Marsh access into the U.S. Air Force chain of command. Finally, with only a half-hour to go, he managed to abort the mission and save us from the horrible irony of having our worst-case fears visited upon us by our own Air Force.

Even as the helicopter evacuation of Brigade 147 from the vicinity of fire support base Hotel drew to a close, it appeared as though yet another Delta situation might be developing. With virtually no other South Vietnamese forces left in Laos to confront, the NVA rapidly increased pressure on Hotel; it appeared to be just a matter of time before reinforcing or resupplying it would become impossible. The looming presence of the towering Co Roc escarpment at the backs of Hotel's defenders also complicated the planning of any orderly land withdrawal. Colonel Lan thought it over, then ordered all forces out of Hotel on his own authority, without seeking permission from I Corps. After all, evacuating the last fire support base left in Laos could have no appreciable impact on the campaign to cut the Ho Chi Minh Trail. Lam Son 719 was over, except for Phase IV, the redeployment of returning units to new locations in South Vietnam. Surely, General Lam could see the logic in that.

But when he found out, General Lam chose not to see the logic in that. And Old Bloody Hands still had an arrow or two left in his quiver. Possibly to save face, or possibly out of pure spite, or both, he ordered Colonel Lan to reoccupy Co Roc immediately, even though such a move made absolutely no tactical sense. This turn of events truly distressed Lan. He was a stickler for discipline, but the very fiber of his soul rebelled at the notion of sending any of his Marines into almost certain death because of poorly thought-out or vindictive orders. He agonized for hours before deciding to send hand-picked, all-volunteer reconnaissance teams—experts at evasion and escape in enemy-held territory—back on to Co Roc. He talked to the teams before they departed as if they were his own sons. In a sense, they truly were.

Colonel Lan had made a tough call, but a good call. The teams survived for more than a week—outmaneuvering NVA patrols and sending back reports—until they were recalled back into Vietnam.

Another unresolved question hung in the air: Would the North Vietnamese momentum carry them across the border, in a major assault against Khe Sanh? There was nothing to stop them or even slow them down anymore, with all South Vietnamese forces withdrawn from Laos. When the U.S. Army's First Brigade of the Fifth Mechanized Division pulled its big artillery pieces and small contingent of tanks away from the border, their mission of supporting Lam Son 719 having been completed, a new emotion rolled in on me. I suddenly began to feel lonely.

A few weeks earlier, the South Vietnamese Marines had been part of a formidable aggregation, on the offensive until the planned withdrawal began. By now, that once-formidable force, weakened and pummeled, was being scattered to the winds, heading for home or other sanctuary—and the Vietnamese Marines had been thrust into the potentially lethal role of a unit left in contact. If the NVA crashed into South Vietnam in hot pursuit, we would have only a screen of light infantry, a severely depleted force of pop-gun 105-mm artillery, and one six-gun battery of 155s to protect the division's command post and its soft logistical underbelly from the flame-throwing tanks of the North Vietnamese.

Would they sustain their momentum, or would they stop at the border? Or if they stopped, would they regroup and continue the attack as soon as possible? Would there be a replay of the hill fights and the siege of the late 1960s?

Whatever they were planning, the NVA had moved their heavy guns within range, and their 122-mm rockets and 130-mm guns could pepper Khe Sanh with impunity, well outside the reach of any counter-battery fire from our 105-mm howitzers. On Co Roc, they had an ideal gunfire spotter's vantage point from which to adjust the fall of shot on the plateau. I wished again that our bunker had a thicker roof, but a few more sandbags wouldn't matter very much, and the time for major reconstruction had long passed. Some of the co-vans in the surrounding hills tried to lighten things up by pretending to adjust NVA incoming fire:

"Shot, over . . . splash! Say, these guys are pretty good. One more move and you're bracketed. . . ."

"The whole world hates a wise ass. Knock it off or I'll give those gunners your coordinates . . . in the clear!" was the not-unexpected response of the command post co-van, who felt as though he was working dead center in the bull's-eye of a large, stationary target.

As time passed, the indirect fire continued, frequently enough to keep us from relaxing but without the sudden increase in intensity that would signal a forthcoming push on the ground.

Midway through this nervous interlude, some mail came in by helicopter. One of my letters was from my alma mater, from the Yale Alumni Fund, to be exact. The Alumni Fund is careful to have its letters signed by a friend or acquaintance from school, whenever possible. So this letter was signed by an attorney named Dick Newman, a classmate from my residential college. Evidently, there was another letter like this one floating around somewhere between Saigon and the Fleet Post Office in San Francisco, because this was the second, or dunning, letter:

Dear John,
I hope the reason I haven't heard from you is not your ill health. . . .

Marvelous! But Dick couldn't have been expected to know that "FPO San Francisco" in my address was a tipoff that I was stationed somewhere in the Far East, and not that I was fighting the Vietnam War from Fisherman's Wharf or the Crazy Horse Saloon, so I could forgive him that bit of unintended irony. My real problem was with Yale, which had thrown its Reserve Officers Training Corps units off campus two years earlier, in the most insulting way its misguided faculty could devise. Troubled by student takeovers and trashing of administrative buildings at Harvard and Columbia, among other places, Yale's president Kingman Brewster had begun to give away pieces of the store, one jump ahead of the students, to keep that from happening in New Haven.

In addition to being cowardly and unpatriotic, the move to abolish ROTC was idiotic, because the original purpose of establishing these units in the colleges and universities was to provide a healthy civilian-trained input to the officer corps of the armed services. This would balance the component from the more isolated service academies and benefit civil-military understanding and relationships. So Brewster and the faculty, in their great wisdom, were cutting off their noses to spite their faces. Yale lost its soul during the Silly Sixties.

Because I could not have afforded a Yale education without the substantial help of my Naval ROTC scholarship, I also considered the school's action a middle-finger salute to people like me, and I was taking it personally. But Dick Newman was a nice guy, and I scribbled a quick reply so it could get out the same day on a resupply helicopter returning to base:

> Dear Dick,
> I have to admit that I am not in the healthiest of circumstances at the moment, but my only real complaint is a persistent, low-grade nausea whenever I read about what's happening in New Haven. . . .

Dick's response came rather quickly, considering the postal delay involved:

> Okay—I know where you are and I'll leave you alone. Write when you have time.

The leisurely enemy shelling continued, heightening our frustration at not being able to hit back with our shorter-range howitzers. On one occasion, however, a co-van was able to inflict some pain and suffering of his own on the Bad Guys. Maj. Bill Dabney, a veteran of the earlier hill fights around Khe Sanh, was driving his jeep in the vicinity of the old U.S. Marine airstrip there when a single artillery round came in, impacting at the south end of the strip, which was marked clearly on his tactical map. From the shape of the crater and his own sensing, he estimated where the fire had come from, pulled out his compass, and shot a back azimuth along that line. Then he drove to the north end of the strip—another precisely marked point on his map—and shot another back azimuth toward the suspected source of fire. Plotted on his map, the two back-azimuth lines intersected in a Laotian valley. So far, so good. Bill Dabney was a field Marine, and one of the bits of field craft he had learned from his father-in-law, the legendary USMC warrior Lewis "Chesty" Puller, was that maps can have memories. From some notations on his three-year-old map, Bill's own memory was jogged into recalling that he had taken fire from that same valley, where NVA troops could roll their big guns out of nearby caves to fire, then roll them back into hiding before the U.S. Marines could find them and react. It was time for some delayed revenge.

A fixed-wing attack aircraft, loaded for bear, soared overhead and Bill was able to contact him by radio, then vector him over to the appropriate valley. Bill heard some dull thuds as the attack pilot unloaded, then a much louder noise as the aviator reported massive secondary explosions. The NVA must have had a lot of ammunition stored in those caves, along with the artillery pieces.

The late John Paul Vann, the prominent and controversial U.S. Army advisor, once remarked that because of its one-year tour policy, America did not have ten years' experience in Vietnam; it had one year's experience times ten. Bill Dabney was a case in point.

It was during this period of waiting for the other shoe to drop that another thought rolled in. Before I left the States, I had tried to buy some more life insurance, to augment my government-issue brand. Because I owned a

Co-van Maj. Bill Dabney proved that old Khe Sanh battle maps can stir up useful memories when he called in an air strike to destroy an NVA artillery position across the border in Laos.

modest New England Life policy, I called the high-school classmate who had sold it to me seven years earlier. A few days later, he called back:

"Why don't you take up something safe, like tightrope walking? Seriously, everybody I've talked to has a war clause, and your being with the Vietnamese Marines instead of staying behind a desk in Saigon doesn't make you an easy sell."

"What about my own policy—does it have a war clause?"

"That's all we're writing these days, but yours predates that. The company would be out of its mind to withhold payment. With the money they'd save, they couldn't *buy* so much bad publicity. The best I can do is increase the value by $5,000 on your next policy anniversary date. You are eligible for an automatic upgrade—no physical exam, no war clause, no questions asked. It just automatically increases and you pay a new premium."

"What's the anniversary date?"

"April first. It will kick in while you are in Vietnam next spring."

With barely a week to go until the anniversary date, I began to think more and more about the need to survive until the first of April, when my wife and children would get an additional five grand (a lot of money back then) if something happened to me. In fact, I may have become a wee bit obsessed about those miserable Northerners having the nerve to even *think* about starting a ground attack before then, thus potentially taking food out of my babies' mouths.

Then the word came down. Not to worry. The division command group and Brigade 147 would be displacing by helilift and motor march to Landing Zone Sharon, five kilometers southwest of Quang Tri City.

The last elements would arrive at Sharon on 1 April 1971.

Chapter 14

By the end of March it appeared that we wouldn't have to hold Khe Sanh at all costs, after all, as the U.S. Marines had to do in 1968. It was the correct decision, to be sure, but until we actually heard it, we could not be certain that a decision to abandon the base would actually be coming down. Our confidence in wise decisions coming down from above had been severely shaken during the past month, with the most recent performance of General Lam with regard to Co Roc being the freshest confidence shaker in memory.

The stark fact was that Khe Sanh, in itself, had no strategic value. It did not lie astride the Ho Chi Minh Trail, fifty kilometers to the west, or even across the much closer routes through the A Shau Valley, which by now had become a virtual superhighway into the South. Historians since have concluded that Gen. William Westmoreland, the former Commander, U.S. Forces, Vietnam, had wanted to hang on to Khe Sanh. He saw it as a possible springboard for a U.S. leap into Laos to cut the Ho Chi Minh Trail, in the vain hope that he could convince President Lyndon Johnson to drop his insistence on "no wider war." For their part, the North Vietnamese since have said that they saw their siege of Khe Sanh as a means of drawing U.S. forces away from Hue and Saigon and other population centers on the coastal plain. It would coincide with the 1968 Tet Offensive, in which they planned to trigger "spontaneous" uprisings against the government throughout South Vietnam.

Any dreams the Northerners might have entertained of repeating their 1954 set-piece-battle victory at Dien Bien Phu, however, were dashed by U.S. air power. Close air support came from both fighter-bombers and the ubiquitous B-52s, acting in a tactical aviation role, whose bombing runs could obliterate three grid squares at a time. The 1968 siege of Khe Sanh kept the beleaguered U.S. Marines in the spotlight for a while, but their losses were minimal compared to those of the NVA, which lost the equivalent of two infantry divisions in their effort to reenact Dien Bien Phu. As soon as U.S. forces reopened Route 9 into Khe Sanh and cleared the area with a ground operation code-named Pegasus, the North Vietnamese drifted away and the Americans abandoned the base, only to reopen it again a couple of years later as another springboard into Laos, this time for the Vietnamese in Lam Son 719.

The current plan called for the Vietnamese Marine division to withdraw behind a screen provided by the Fifty-fourth ARVN Regiment and the U.S. First Brigade of the Fifth Mechanized Division, to relocate in eastern Quang Tri Province. As planned, Brigade 147 and the Marine Division command group displaced to landing zone Sharon, five kilometers southwest of Quang Tri City, with the last units arriving there on 1 April. Brigade 258 left Khe Sanh two days later, taking over an area of operations near Mai Loc, halfway back to Quang Tri. The following day, Brigade 369 moved out to an area of operations adjacent to Brigade 147's.

Before the move-out was complete, Colonel Tief and I managed to take a pair of semi-exciting helicopter rides. The first was a spur-of-the-moment afternoon aerial reconnaissance of the Khe Sanh area. Since all the Marines had returned from Laos by then, there was no reason to fly over Laotian territory; indeed, we were not authorized to cross into Laos. As we flew along the western edge of the Khe Sanh base area, we were looking to the east, where Route 9 left the plateau and began to meander back into South Vietnam. Then I glanced straight down, my attention caught by a flash of sunlight reflected off some water we were passing over. Water? The only water around there was the river that separated South Vietnam from Laos. And that was the river, and we were on the wrong side of it, heading deeper into Laos.

I turned around to look out of the other side of the helicopter, and my legs reacted as though I had just stepped on a rattlesnake, driving me upward out of my canvas-webbed seat. We were cruising leisurely along the rocky cliff-like face of Co Roc, which was dotted with caves. Any of these caves could have contained bad guys with weapons, lots of them. But they wouldn't have needed much in the way of weaponry. We were so close that a couple of well-thrown rocks could have knocked us out of the sky. Colonel Tief took one look at Co Roc, then turned his gaze toward the young Army warrant officer pilot, with a "Where do we get such men?" look on his face. The look was not pleasant to behold.

I got my legs working and stumbled to the front of the UH-1, where I tapped the pilot on the shoulder, pointed back toward Khe Sanh, and started jabbing insistently with my forefinger in that direction. He shrugged, still clueless, and started to bring us around. It did not take long to get back across the border, but it seemed like a thousand years. I could not see Co Roc any more, so I just hunkered down and waited for the first series of bullet holes to open silently in the bird, followed by the sound of enemy gunfire. But that shoe did not drop, and to this day I still do not know what forces, if any, the NVA had on Co Roc. They must have had some artillery forward observers up there, at a minimum. We had recon teams up there, but during daylight hours they probably were way under cover.

Our second helicopter adventure actually occurred as we debarked at the Khe Sanh helipad, after flying back from a trip to the new division command post near Quang Tri to see how the relocation was going. Almost as though they knew who was coming, the NVA artillerymen greeted us with a twelve-gun salute at the moment the helicopter's skids touched the ground. As we moved toward the command bunker at a brisk pace, I saw mute evidence that the indirect-fire attacks had been stepped up and were inflicting more damage within the combat base. The most conspicuous casualty was the co-vans' outhouse—a two-holer dedicated in a double-ring ceremony the previous month—which had suffered a direct, noisome hit.

Inside the bunker, I unfolded my map so we could track the progress of the redeployment with the co-vans still on the scene. Within a few minutes, two rounds landed close enough to rattle our cage with a very loud bang. The concussion knocked some red clay soil from the overhead timbers, and some of it landed on my unfolded map, which now seemed to be functioning as a drop cloth. We all looked at each other, but nobody said anything. As I tilted my map and let the new layer of soil slide off, I couldn't shake the feeling of how unreal all of this was, like a cliché scene from a World War I trench-warfare movie. At least it was past 1 April, and I had moved past my angst lest my extra five thousand dollars of life insurance not kick in. But I still wished that the bunker had a thicker roof.

I was so convinced that they were reading our minds by this time that I half expected to receive another twelve-gun departure salute at the helipad. But it didn't happen. The North Vietnamese *must* have been pretty badly hurt by Lam Son 719. Otherwise they could and would have made the Marine Division's exit from Khe Sanh much more difficult by applying severe ground pressure to go with the indirect-fire attacks. In any event, the redeployment took place without any major hitches or delays.

Landing Zone Sharon and the brigade operating areas were not exactly safe havens. Two nights after its arrival, Brigade 147 underwent a mortar attack near Sharon, and two nights after that, the Fourth Battalion fought off a platoon-sized ground probe, at a cost of two Marines killed in action and three wounded. The NVA left behind ten dead, or so it seemed at first. In the overcast morning's half-light we went to the scene of the fight, where the NVA bodies lay in front of the tactical wire, stiffening in death. They wore black, collarless, long-sleeved shirts and short pants, and were barefoot. Their lower extremities were caked in mud, as though they had waded through soggy fields or paddies to approach the VNMC positions with maximum stealth. As I walked past one body, lying on its side, I sensed some kind of movement—a pulse, maybe—with my peripheral vision, and nearly jumped out of my skin. This guy was still alive!

We rolled him over, and he hadn't stiffened one bit in the hours since the attack. We could see the small bullet-entry hole, ringed with purple, in his forehead at first, but when we rolled him we could see a much larger exit hole, with brains pushing out. This had relieved the pressure inside his skull, which certainly would have killed him by now if the skull had not been forced open by the exiting bullet.

We called for stretcher bearers and a jeep, to get this nearly dead man to the nearest aid station. By early afternoon, he had been stabilized and transferred to a. field hospital nearby, and we went to see him. He was sitting up and chattering like a chipmunk about everything: his home, his family and friends, and his unit and all its activities. There was no stopping after disclosing only name, rank, and serial number for this guy. I tried to remember which cultures were the ones where anyone saving another's life was obligated to take care of the person he saved, forever. Maybe this young soldier thought he had just hit the gravy train; he certainly was genuinely happy about his good fortune. At any rate, for all his talking he didn't know enough to reveal any major battle plans. Still, we did get the impression from him that enemy forces were widely scattered in the eastern part of Quang Tri Province, and probing actions like his platoon's were not the harbinger of a major attack anywhere, anytime soon.

So we still had to maintain vigilant security around our positions, and keep patrols moving through the area, but otherwise we could go into a semi-standdown. We sorely needed one. We had to regroup, replace people, repair weapons and equipment, restore depleted stocks of supplies and ammunition, and most of all, sit down and think through everything that had happened over the past month or so. That was the only way to help ensure that when the South Vietnamese Marines went into their next big battle—and more were coming—they would be more the masters of events and less the prisoners of them. As co-vans, we could do a lot more for our Vietnamese counterparts than just coordinating and directing U.S. fire support. Stepping beyond that limited role could bring about our greatest contribution to these valiant Marines.

But we had some severe cultural hurdles to overcome.

The first was the Commander Syndrome. All warrior cultures place a massive amount of faith, sometimes unwarranted, in the power of their commanders to guide their warfighters to victory and to bring them home safely. But the Vietnamese, from whatever ancient feudal precedents, were

Col. Bui The Lan, commanding the Vietnamese Marine division in the field, talks to troops at their outpost adjacent to Landing Zone Sharon, near Quang Tri City, after the conclusion of Lam Son 719.

carrying the Cult of the Commander to an illogical extreme. Before Lam Son 719, the supreme field commanders in the VNMC were the three brigade commanders. They ran their own operations; ran their supply support efforts; and ran their personnel fiefdoms with the carrot and stick of both promotions and disciplinary action, to say nothing of the pay their troops received or failed to receive.

Despite all this authority, the brigade commanders brought relatively few trappings of power to the field. Their command posts were far less cumbersome than the U.S. equivalents, and also less capable. In great measure, this was because the mechanisms for controlling artillery, naval gunfire, and air support and coordinating such fire support with subordinate units' maneuvers were either scaled down or lacking altogether. After all, that was one of the things the co-vans were supposed to do. Similarly, the staff sections were sparsely manned, by U.S. standards, and did not work in anywhere near the detail. As long as the resupply helicopters got out to the battalions on schedule every four days, for example, the S-4 logistics officer generally was regarded as doing his job properly. There was no need for staff sections to prepare plans, reports, and requisitions to go to the next higher echelon, because brigade was the biggest dog around. The next higher echelon, back in Saigon, had little interest in all the tactical details of operations they did not control directly.

Similarly, the brigade commanders showed little inclination to micromanage the activities of their subordinate battalions, which quite often operated independently. When covering large areas against relatively light opposition, as in search-and-clear operations, for example, the battalions themselves would split into two forces, one headed by the commander and the other by the battalion executive officer.

All up and down the line, then, the Vietnamese Marine commanders were accustomed to operating independently, with little in the way of detailed staff input or requirements to submit plans, make reports, or request combat or logistical support that was out of the ordinary. Up through brigade level, the commanders often ran their operations out of their hip pockets, one level up, on the average, from what the co-vans were accustomed to seeing. That is, a Vietnamese battalion command post was not much more sophisticated than that of a U.S. Marine rifle company; and a Vietnamese brigade command post was significantly smaller and less complex than a U.S. infantry battalion's headquarters setup for extended operations in the field.

In the U.S. Marines, platoon leaders and, at times, company commanders ran things out of their hip pockets, but battalion commanders and higher who tried to do this usually rendered their units ineffective and destroyed themselves in the process. Trying to stay on top of absolutely everything, they insisted on monitoring all subordinate units directly, writing up or approving all plans and reports personally, and unilaterally making all major tactical decisions with regard to maneuver and fire support. Amid the artificialities of training or unit-evaluation exercises back in the States, commanders could sometimes get away with this Superman posture for three or four sleepless nights and days, until the exercise concluded with them standing triumphantly atop a final objective of some sort. In extended land combat, however, reality sets in after several days. Battalion commanders generally come to realize that they lack the ability to be in more than one place at one time. They also discover that surviving with one's judgment intact becomes problematic after a week of little or no sleep. (After all, no one expects the captain to remain on the bridge of his ship all day, every day, for the duration of his cruise.) Seizing an objective is never a reason to relax, either. Instead, it is a mandate to consolidate, regroup, and either continue the attack or dig in to repel a counterattack.

Faced with their own human frailties, the seasoned commanders loosen the reins a bit and let their executive officers function as more chiefs of staff than as second-in-command. They let the S-3 operations officer "fight" the battalion, prepare reports, and make plans for subsequent operations. They let the fire support coordinator actually coordinate supporting fires and air strikes; and they let the S-4 logistics officer make timely decisions to meet the battalion's material needs. The commanders who fail to let go are setting themselves up for their own relief for cause, sooner rather than later. That's because, sooner or later, through fatigue-impaired judgment or inability to cover all their bets at the same time, they will botch something badly enough for worried senior commanders to pull the plug on them.

But the hard lessons that U.S. Marine officers had to learn by the time they assumed battalion command did not emerge clearly within the Vietnamese Marine Corps frame of reference until they tried to go to the field as a division for the first time. Until then, a Cult of the Commander prevailed, usually with great success in the field environment of the time. The commanders called all the shots, and the staff officers rendered some assistance but more often stayed out of the way, ever fearing to question their leaders' judgment on any matter. Such deference to authority led to the spectacle of five, to fifteen, to thirty officers, depending upon the level of command, waiting for orders instead of taking the initiative to help their boss by collecting and analyzing information from above and below, fine-tuning battle plans as the situation deepened, or suggesting alternate courses of action if the unit ran into difficulties. Thus for the commander it was sink or swim. As long as he continued to win, he would be a hero—indeed, a minor deity. But once he began to lose, he would have no one to blame but himself and his reputation would plummet, disintegrating into ashes. It was a case of winning big or losing bigger.

Brigade 147 was under the most pressure by far during Lam Son 719, and it was here that the shortcomings of the old way, under perhaps the most experienced and hitherto successful of all the brigade commanders, were thrown into stark relief. Each of the three battalions, when operating outside the confines of fire support base Delta, marched to its own drum. Even though contact with the enemy was nearly continuous, the brigade command group was unwilling or unable to coordinate the battalions' actions into a mutually supporting maneuver. Indeed, when the Fourth and Seventh Battalions fell back on Delta prior to the final NVA assault, they hunkered down in their own defensive positions rather than undertaking an aggressive effort to clear the western slope of the firebase, a mission that should have been directed and coordinated by Brigade 147.

Clearing the slopes of NVA antiaircraft gunners was the VNMC's only chance to conduct an aerial resupply of Delta and eventually to conduct an orderly withdrawal from Delta, possibly even an aerial evacuation, as was the case with fire support base Hotel. Division headquarters had the means to provide artillery support to the two battalions as they fell back on Delta and to support any subsequent sweep operations to clear the slopes. However, they were stymied by the brigade commander's inability or refusal to provide the battalions' scheme of maneuver, an absolute prerequisite for any fire support plan, and his flat refusal to bring in artillery or air strikes within a thousand meters of his position. To be sure, there was reason for him to be distrustful of the skill of Vietnamese Marine artillerymen trying to operate in this rugged terrain (three earlier air strikes had mistakenly dropped on his own troops), but his otherwise logical fears had become irrational under these extreme circumstances. The Commander Syndrome had kicked in with numbing severity, paralyzing an experienced professional into near-fatal inaction. Only when the division commander overrode the brigade commander's objections and approved a general fire support plan was much-needed artillery brought in, effectively stopping the first NVA assault on Delta.

The brigades did not have the market cornered with regard to the Commander Syndrome. Operating without a chief of staff, the division commander tended to micromanage too much at first, instead of staying focused on larger concerns. This led to staff officers bucking relatively easy and minor decisions—for example, when should a co-van bunker be built, and by whom?—all the way to the top. Toward the end of the operation, as the G-3 began to take on some of the chief of staff functions, things improved.

Not-so-faint echoes of the Commander Syndrome could be found within the staff sections, as well. Even in as complex an enterprise as G-4 logistics operations, junior officers who should have been making timely decisions to keep things running would cause unconscionable delays by waiting for the approval of the principal staff officer. This was exacerbated by the fact that the real G-4 stayed in Saigon, working on the high-priority project of taking over the Di An base camp, recently abandoned by departing U.S. Army units. His understudy up north lacked the confidence of his boss in dealing with subordinate units, other division staff sections, and higher headquarters, and his diffidence contributed greatly to the paralysis. Even such mundane activities as digging bunkers in the Khe Sanh command post became mini-crises and brought unacceptable delays before they were accomplished.

Old habits die hard, and the Cult of the Commander was so well established that it would be exceedingly difficult even to dent, much less to eradicate. As we co-vans compared notes from our separate experiences during Lam Son 719, clear patterns of behavior began to emerge, and solutions began to suggest themselves.

First, however, we had to figure out what was actually going on. Nobody, from the commanders on down, was trying to shoot himself in the foot. Everyone was clinging to patterns of behavior that had worked, sometimes spectacularly, in the past. But all of a sudden they were in a new game, with a new enemy, on a different court, with new rules, and a new playbook. Moreover, they were playing as part of a new team, whose organization, slowly taking shape, was still unformed.

Certainly, part of the difficulty in overcoming the Commander Syndrome lay in allaying the fear felt by subordinates when approaching commanders with new or different ideas about how things should be done. Some commanders—Major Do Huu Tung of the Sixth Battalion, for example—were such aristocrats and such masters of the Imperial Whine that they could terrify anyone who approached, even with a good idea. And anyone who dared approach with a bad idea was dead meat from the start.

The trick, then, was not only to make the commanders more approachable, but also to make certain that they would be approached with good ideas and suggestions. The staff officers and subordinate commanders had to learn what to say, and to have confidence in it, before they could be induced to put their necks on the line. And the page was blank, so the co-vans had to help fill it up with good ideas.

Few, if any, of us had even seen the inside of a U.S. Marine division-level command post, or even a regimental one, except as visitors. Still, we had access to field manuals and operational publications, and we had some understanding of what worked for the South Vietnamese and what did not. We felt equal to the task of cobbling something together which, although it might not be the perfect solution, would be a lot better than what we had at present.

In the cynical characterization by Lt. Tom Kiefer in Herman Wouk's classic, *The Caine Mutiny*, the U.S. Navy was "designed by geniuses to be run by idiots." We were nowhere near the genius level in military affairs, and the South Vietnamese were nowhere near being idiots. We were learning something new from them almost every day. Our job was to capture the wisdom of the ages—or as much of it as we could comprehend—and put it in writing for them. We had to begin writing things down, to get everyone working off a common sheet of music. When everyone understands the baseline for any improvisations, it becomes easier to improvise. This meant developing a set of standing operating procedures (SOPs) that could provide a starting point for most operations.

On the operational side of things, the biggest problem we faced was that the newly formed division headquarters tended to react to events, rather than control them. Deploying without any prior experience or even training exercises in running a tactical operations center in the field, they were winging it. The habit of deference to the brigade commanders, ingrained in Saigon, essentially robbed the operations center of any decision-making capability. In effect, it was little more than a supporting arms coordination center, and an imperfect one, at that.

Further maintaining this hands-off attitude, division representatives—and especially the division commander—did not see fit to visit their deployed brigades to gather firsthand information and impressions. Not once. And the brigades seldom sent anyone back to the division, to keep abreast of the larger picture. They did not seem to want to talk to each other, when talking to each other was the key to victory or even survival. This mutual standoff killed effective control from division of both tactical maneuver and fire support planning. The "let brigade run it" attitude was a killer.

It was time for an attitude check.

To beat that lingering attitude back to parade rest, we needed something, in the form of an SOP or other directive document, signed by the boss, Lieutenant General Khang, that would mandate the primacy of the division over the brigades. Having done that, the document would spell out the organization and functioning of the division command group and the tactical operations center, with clearly defined planning and reporting requirements that were mandatory, not optional.

In terms of combat support, the weak link was clearly the artillery, whose shortcomings had been masked by relatively benign operating conditions in the Delta and even the Middle Region, west of Da Nang and An Hoa. Down south, the sun (almost) always shone and the terrain was flat, providing ideal conditions for any cannon-cocker. Along the Demilitarized Zone and into Laos, the rugged terrain and heavy weather demanded an ability to include terrain and weather in any calculations sent to the guns. It wasn't there.

This deficiency led to a larger problem. Lacking confidence in their own direct-support artillery, and fearing that friendly rounds would land amid their own Marines, the ground commanders held out for fixed-wing close air support or helicopter gunships for counterbattery work. These are relatively inefficient ways to go after enemy artillery. Artillery battalion commanders took on the aura of independence of their infantry brigade commanders, and effective organization and control of fires from division level became impossible.

Combat losses exacerbated the problem. After being forced to spike its guns on Delta and to escape and evade with the infantry units into South

Vietnam, the Second Artillery Battalion ceased to exist. Those who made it back to Khe Sanh (most of the battalion, actually) did not regroup, as the riflemen of Brigade 147 had done. Instead, they moved into the hooches of their friends at Khe Sanh and dropped out of sight. It took nearly two weeks to begin to reconstitute the Second Artillery Battalion, and follow-on instruction would have to go all the way back to the basics: "This is a 105-mm howitzer. . . ."

Next, a strong division artillery section would have to be created, with a commander who could function both as a principal staff advisor to the division commander and as someone with command authority over the artillery battalion commanders. In a glaring example of the Commander Syndrome that paralleled that of the infantry units, the artillery battalion commanders maintained attitudes of autonomy that the artillery officers at division were unwilling to challenge. The division artillery concept would have to be backed by an SOP, prepared at division level, which would prescribe uniform procedures for all battalions. The SOP would establish fire-direction centers at battalion level as the primary technical fire-direction agencies. The centers would increase the battalions' proficiency through frequent drills and command-post exercises.

Also at artillery battalion level, a strong S-2 intelligence section would be needed to maintain target lists, develop target intelligence, and record and analyze damage assessments, among other things. Forward observers would be permanently assigned to infantry battalions and rifle companies, ending the haphazard practices of Lam Son 719, which sometimes caused observers to join their infantry units at the last minute with neither maps nor radios, the primary tools of their trade.

Finally, periodic testing would be required, to check familiarity with firing procedures, and periodic firepower demonstrations would have to be conducted to display capabilities and restore the Marines' confidence in their own artillery—that loss of confidence being one of the biggest casualties of Lam Son 719.

The absence of the G-4 logistics officer from the Khe Sanh command post, coupled with a paucity of written guidance through orders, plans, forms, and SOPs, made the combat service support aspects of the operation run a lot rougher than anyone's worst expectations. The relatively junior and inexperienced acting G-4 was reluctant to demonstrate his inexperience by trying to coordinate with—or make requests or demands of, or require reports from, or make liaison with—subordinate combat service support units, division or brigade staff sections, I Corps headquarters, or his supporting logistic command at higher echelons. What we had here was a failure to communicate, big-time.

The situation was exacerbated by the fact that no one else in the G-4 section seemed to have either the technical expertise or the authority to give the acting G-4 a much-needed hand. If a question arose regarding engineering, communications, supply, or motor transport, for example, it first had to be taken to the acting G-4 himself, who then would refer it to the commander of the element that provided that particular service. These commanders knew the answers but could not commit themselves and their people to a solution without the authority of—that's right—the acting G-4 or, sometimes, the division commander if the acting G-4 still felt underempowered. This merry minuet could start up over the most routine of activities, such as assembling working parties to load or unload helicopters. Sometimes it took so long to find anyone with the authority to organize a loading party that the helicopters had to shut down and wait in the landing zone, vulnerable to the enemy's long-range guns.

From the outset of Lam Son 719, guidance from I Corps was that the VNMC division should function with minimal U.S. supply support. But advisors at all levels were pressured to use U.S. channels to get support that was not flowing through Vietnamese channels. At the same time, the Vietnamese displayed a great unwillingness or inability to consider co-van suggestions in practically any technical area—until things got so bad that the problem could not be solved without going to an advisor.

A lot of this confusion and angst could have been avoided with a few strategic pieces of paper, beginning with an administration and logistics order, to accompany the division's operations order. If there was one for Lam Son 719, it was not in evidence. Such a directive would have designated, among many other things, the units to provide specific types of supply and maintenance support. Without something like it, there were significant delays at the beginning of the operation, as advisors and others scrambled around Khe Sanh, looking for "the lance corporal with the keys"—trying to determine who would be doing what for whom. Such a basic order would also have included a "reports required" section, which would have mandated a daily logistics summary from each brigade. A junior division staff officer would not have needed to beg the brigade commanders for reports of their logistical requirements on a daily basis. Another document, called the "helicopter mission assignment table," would have eliminated a great deal of confusion, but no such table was on hand until the co-vans created one out of sheer necessity.

In general, the VNMC division's motor transport capability covered the motor marches to and from Khe Sanh, but Lam Son 719 clearly showed that they lacked a deployable maintenance capability. This did not come back to haunt us during the operation, but it threatened bad things to come. As the character in the old oil-filter commercial explains, "Pay me now or pay me later." Perhaps we needed additional logistical advisor support at brigade and battalion level, where almost all the co-vans were focused on operational considerations instead of logistical ones, where the Vietnamese actually needed the most advice and support.

Fortunately, the brightest spot in the logistics picture proved to be the well-organized and well-staffed medical services. The Collecting and Clearing Company, which provided the initial screening point for casualties, was up and running immediately upon its arrival at Khe Sanh. The air evacuation of casualties worked smoothly, and the wounded were handled most professionally by Vietnamese Marine doctors and hospital corpsmen at all echelons. By the time the VNMC division had returned to Quang Tri and Mai Loc, nearly six hundred wounded and sick Marines had moved successfully through the evacuation chain all the way back to our hospital at the Thu Duc training center. This was life-or-death stuff, and the medics came through like champions.

In the aftermath of Lam Son 719, we had an immense task ahead of us. The job of rebuilding the division would have been daunting enough with the cheery cooperation of our Vietnamese counterparts every step of the way, and nobody was naive enough to count on that. Criticism, no matter how constructive and well meant, is seldom well received, even under the best of circumstances. And these circumstances were definitely—by a great margin—not the best.

For one thing, the Marine Division (especially Brigade 147) had been slapped around a lot, even though the punishment they inflicted far exceeded the punishment they endured. So a certain amount of finger-pointing, leading only to denial and defensiveness, was inevitable. This was no time to come waltzing in like Pollyanna, bringing long lists of suggestions for self-improvement. It was nearly a certainty that, in the areas where improvement was most needed, it would be most stoutly resisted. There was even an aphorism about it:

The amount of effort expended to deny error
is directly proportional to the size of the error.

The concept of "face" also came into play here. Vietnamese commanders at all levels had an ingrained reluctance to be seen as relying too heavily on the advice of their co-vans. Recognizing this, many of us had adopted an indirect approach. We would toss out a new idea or suggestion casually (almost too casually). It would be received with benign indifference and left to sit on the table for a while. Then, after an appropriate amount of time had expired, our Vietnamese counterparts might revisit the issue or the area of discussion, play with the new idea for a while, and, if they liked it, eventually reintroduce it as their own original thought. Fine.

The subtle approach generally worked for nice little gems and nuggets of ideas, when there was no requirement for immediate action or decision making. But how could we continue to use this face-saving (for our counterparts), indirect technique of persuasion when practically everything needed fixing simultaneously and immediately?

Face is not just about embarrassment; face is about power and perceptions of who has it and who doesn't in any given situation. A combat commander who loses face, especially when his personal and professional competence is at issue, can see his power as an effective leader be undercut severely or evaporate altogether. Therefore, it would be unrealistic to expect Lieutenant General Khang or even a newly appointed Brigadier General Lan to sign a shiny, new sweeping directive that corrected all the Marine Division's shortcomings. That would have been a tacit admission that all those shortcomings were in fact present on their watch. Thus, even though the ultimate goal was to have everyone doing things correctly and in a coordinated way, getting their guidance from the same sheet of music, we would have to continue moving carefully along the way. Working through indirection, with deliberate haste, we needed to take the raucous jam session of improvisation currently playing and turn it into a powerful symphony of coordinated effort.

We also needed the Vietnamese to pick up some of the too-hard functions—such as organizing, coordinating, and controlling tactical and logistical helicopter lift at division level—that they had left to the co-vans by default. A bucket of worms that came with going to the field as a division for the first time, these functions constituted a complex, though controllable, new endeavor. New opportunities for foul-ups and losing face presented themselves with every passing hour. Inevitably this risk played into the basic reluctance of most of the Vietnamese to work outside of their own backyards—their own self-acknowledged areas of expertise—to begin with. Running all those birds and keeping all those troops and all that cargo sorted out was the equivalent of asking them to take a brand-new job in a foreign country. The prevailing attitude seemed to be, "Let the co-vans be the ones to lose face when things didn't work." There was little concern for the overriding objective: to get the division up and running on all cylinders, with all hands pulling together and no one trying to cut himself any slack.

Weakness in identifying the proper objective and then keeping it in sight appeared again and again throughout the Vietnamese chain of command, military and civilian.

Objective is one of the nine principles of war. Obviously, any plan to move against enemy forces requires a final objective—the ultimate goal of the battle—with several intermediate objectives whose seizure will support the drive to the final objective. These intermediate objectives also serve as milestones to mark progress toward the final objective and at times to signal the shift to a new phase of the operation.

For too many Vietnamese commanders and staff officers, however, selecting objectives meant little more than making a series of neat little circles on a map. If such objectives do not contribute to the final accomplishment of the mission, however, they soon lose their meaning. And when the meaning is bled out of objectives, the entire operation loses its sense of purpose. In the case of the Vietnamese Marines in particular, advisors learned to recognize the point in an operation when an infectious "back to Saigon" mood would set in. About that time, the operation's final objective would seem to evaporate and the new goal would be one of disengaging and getting as many Marines as possible back safely from the operation.

Failure to recognize the significance of the objective plagued Lam Son 719 at the highest levels. As originally conceived, the plan was either to seize control of the Ho Chi Minh Trail or to rupture it so badly that the NVA and Vietcong forces operating in the South would run precariously short of supplies and equipment. The net effect, it was hoped, would be similar to the results of the ground incursion into Cambodia and the neutralization of Sihanoukville as the port of entry for supplies brought by sea from the North. Enemy forces in South Vietnam's IV Corps region were essentially starved out of business long enough for U.S. forces to disengage and leave the country without undue military pressure. In a military sense, the operation was a highly successful spoiling attack. In a larger strategic sense, of course, the Cambodian operation accomplished exactly what the North Vietnamese had wanted. It facilitated the removal of a major piece of the American military presence from South Vietnam, so that the Northerners could deal with the Southerners in their own way.

Had Lieutenant General Lam's I Corps forces stayed the course for perhaps another hard month of fighting, as General Abrams had urged, the outcome of Lam Son 719 might have been markedly different, even decisive in the outcome of the war. But President Thieu showed misgivings when the first casualty reports began to come in. He stalled the thrust barely twenty kilometers into Laos, leaving time for North Vietnamese defenders to gather their forces and for bad weather to arrive. After I Corps got restarted, the eventual walk through a deserted Tchepone was anticlimactic and did little more than to kick off a disorderly and costly South Vietnamese withdrawal under pressure. Before long, news photos of terrified South Vietnamese soldiers clinging to the skids of medical evacuation helicopters in a desperate bid for personal safety became the media's predominant symbol for Lam Son 719, published and broadcast around the world. Those dramatic pictures were a grave disservice to many brave South Vietnamese troops who fought their way out of Laos, inflicting more punishment on the enemy than they took, but the power of those compelling images prevailed.

Similarly, in the VNMC's part of Lam Son 719 south of Route 9, there were key spots within the operational area that the enemy showed great fear of losing. These were the logical objectives. Instead, the Marine Division's operations order talked of such general objectives as destroying enemy equipment and supply caches, and only of *trying* to seize the vital intersection of Route 14 and Route 22. All they had to do was try. It didn't even have to be a particularly strong try.

The likelihood of failure was made a certainty by sending in an understrength brigade (minus one of its three battalions, left behind to defend fire support base Delta) to make the attempt. To further ensure failure,

These American newsmen flew out to Khe Sanh to talk to the Vietnamese Marine division commander—but he didn't want to talk to them.

that particular brigade was receiving rock-bottom priority for air and artillery support from I Corps—in other words, virtually none. Its situation did not change until all the ARVN units were out of Laos. By then the brigade had moved back to the vicinity of Delta for a last-ditch defense, which proved as uncoordinated as their earlier aimless wandering. It was small wonder that the Vietnamese Marines accomplished little, if anything, that had to do with the original objectives of Lam Son 719, other than inflicting more casualties than they suffered in a battle of attrition.

There was one more cultural impediment that was a potential show-stopper in building the combat efficiency of the Marine Division. By inclination and training, we co-vans tended to be systems oriented. We sought to establish habits, procedures, and systems that would enable the Vietnamese Marines to move into new surroundings and face new situations and carry out new missions, despite all the accompanying uncertainties. We wanted our Vietnamese counterparts to step forward and seize new responsibilities with confidence whenever the situation demanded, following a trail of written guidance about where to begin, rather than staying in their own backyards of military expertise. We also sought to ingrain, through training, useful patterns of service and operations that would help them withstand the rough shocks of war and continue to function effectively. Finally, we wanted them to understand and appreciate all the ways in which they could support each other and strengthen the team. Yes, we wanted to turn that jam session into a powerful symphony concert.

On the other hand, the Vietnamese, to the extent that they still paid homage to the Cult of the Commander, did not see fitting themselves into systems and patterns as all that important. It was the commander, with his knowledge, courage, good instincts, and good luck, with possibly the Mandate of Heaven thrown in, who was all-important. Systems were things to be either used or circumvented, for the benefit of the commander or his family, or perhaps his unit, in some cases. So it was not realistic to expect Vietnamese commanders to convert instantly to cookbook leadership, no matter how many great ideas we might manage to set down on paper.

Despite all the cultural, professional, and personal reasons suggesting that any rapid and major reform effort within the Marine Division was destined to fail, occasional glimmers of hope refused to die out completely. From time to time, an action or remark by one of our Vietnamese counterparts provided evidence that they were giving at least some of our ideas some thought, if not quite taking them on board yet. And every once in a great while, something more dramatic would happen.

A case in point: While Brigade 258 was in the midst of moving from Khe Sanh to Mai Loc, Lieutenant Colonel Luong and I flew back to I Corps headquarters at Dong Ha, to work out the boundaries of the brigade's new tactical area of responsibility. Then we flew directly to Mai Loc, where Luong spread out his map and briefed Lt. Col. Nguyen Thanh Tri, the brigade commander.

Colonel Tri was not pleased with his assigned area.

In fact, Colonel Tri was downright unhappy about it and let Luong know in no uncertain terms. Tri disliked the fact that a major road ran through his area and that his people would have to sweep it for mines each morning before any traffic could roll. And he wanted to be closer to a village, where his troops could go into town for liberty in the evenings. And so on. And so on. So, he concluded, with a couple of dismissive backhand waves, why didn't we just go back to I Corps and coordinate him a new and improved area?

I glanced at Luong. He was crushed. Tri was only a lieutenant colonel, just like Luong, but he was a very senior lieutenant colonel holding a full colonel's command billet, and everyone knew that he was about to be promoted. Further, Tri was highly respected throughout the Vietnamese Marine Corps and had brought his brigade through Lam Son 719 with relatively few casualties and his excellent professional reputation intact. Moreover, to add to his stature, Nguyen Thanh Tri was a highly popular singer in South Vietnam, with several of his recordings listed among the top hits of the day. And for good measure, his troops loved him.

So Luong, an obscure lieutenant colonel staff pogue, was dealing with an unholy combination of Gen. George S. Patton and Frank Sinatra. Luong had a look on his face like that of a puppy that had just been kicked by a master he had trusted.

This was getting dangerous. The Commander Syndrome was being replayed in full color and wraparound sound, right before my eyes. I don't know which got to me more—Luong's hurt and submissive demeanor, or Tri's evident delight in playing King of the Hill one more time and buffalo-ing a staff officer from division. He knew that he was going against everything we had been trying to do in getting the Vietnamese Marines to function as a division, but he was determined to fight a rear-guard action, just for the hell of it.

It was time for Nguyen Thanh Patton/Sinatra Tri to go to school.

I drew Luong off to one side, out of Tri's earshot. I tried to keep my voice down, but I was steaming, and it probably came out like a hiss: "If you go back to I Corps and coordinate him a new area, you will never be a G-3!"

Luong looked startled. Now he was getting it from both sides, and he hadn't expected that from me.

I pressed on. "I Corps has set those boundaries and Colonel Lan has approved them, by the authority he has vested in you. Lieutenant Colonel Tri has no authority to demand that they be changed, to satisfy his personal whim."

Luong continued to stare at me, wide-eyed. Maybe I was beginning to get through. Time to press on some more: "When you speak as the G-3, you speak for Colonel Lan. You speak with his full authority. The brigade commanders must obey the orders you transmit to them, even though they may be senior to you. If they do not like their orders, they can explain why to Colonel Lan, because they are his orders."

Luong was beginning to nod his head a little. Everyone knew that anyone questioning Colonel Lan's orders face-to-face was likely to lose so much face that he would closely resemble the Headless Horseman. It was time for the final shot: "If you don't believe me, call Colonel Lan and ask him yourself. He will not be happy to hear that his orders are being questioned and defied."

Luong nodded again, then turned on his heel and left the room. I hoped he was looking for his radio operator, to call Colonel Lan.

A few minutes later, he returned with a tight smile on his face. I knew instantly: Lan had backed him up. Luong went directly to Tri and told him that his area assignment would stand, and if he had any problems with it

This statue at the entrance to a Saigon cemetery invites all interred there to rest after a job well done.

he was free to take them up with Colonel Lan, who had approved the assignment.

Tri's face and manner darkened, but the storm clouds blew over as he began to contemplate a head-butting encounter with Lan, which Tri would surely lose.

Luong had acted upon the new message and carried the day. But would it last?

By the next day, it was clear. Luong walked around the division command post with new confidence, bordering on cockiness. He acted as though a hundred-pound weight had been lifted from his shoulders. In fact, he became difficult, bordering on impossible, for a while as he reveled in his newly discovered power. Then he settled down a bit, but not all the way down.

Laughing Larry Luong had seen the light. Among the key staff officers of the Marine division, he had stepped up to the plate, stroked the ball, and now was rounding third base, heading for home.

If Laughing Larry was coming home, others must follow, in time.

There was hope—a lot of it.

The tour ended quickly, in an unexpected way.

Contrary to my own experience and subsequent expectations, I was not destined to be standing in a helicopter landing zone, with my faded, paper-thin tiger suit pasted against my gaunt frame by the rotor blast, waiting to present my bewildered successor with a map packet and a smile. Instead, I was sunning myself on a large flat rock near Quang Tri when the morning single-sideband radio call from Saigon came through.

Marsh Carter's voice came in, filtered and distorted through the airways:

"Yoouur wiiife haaas juuust founnnd theee perrfect houuse in Aar-linnngtonnn. Is it Ohhh Kaaay . . . O-verrr?"

"What the hell. . . . O-ver?" Marsh always had a way of getting my undivided attention in a hurry.

Marsh outlined things succinctly, fighting through the radio's distortion. My change-of-station orders were in. I was going to Headquarters Marine Corps, and leaving Vietnam two weeks early, to make a contact relief with a major in the Chief of Staff's office. Someone in Personnel had tipped off my wife in Norfolk, and she had already found a place close to Headquarters, a custom-built brick colonial, thirty years old, for fifty grand. So what's the answer?

That was a lot of information to process in a hurry. I was raised in the Washington, D.C., area, so it would be good to get back. The house had to be something similar to my parents' house in Bethesda, though about seven years older. They worked long hours at Headquarters, so being close by was important, and this house met any realtor's top three priorities: Location, location, and location. The Army's Fort Myer, with all its facilities, including commissary, post exchange, and officers' club, was another nearby plus.

My wife had a power of attorney that was comprehensive enough to move things forward, although I would be back there in time to sign everything at settlement—but not in time to change very much if I didn't like what I saw. This was the first house we'd ever bought, and I sensed that there were dozens of potential pitfalls that I didn't know enough to worry about. But if I put a hold on everything, we would lose this house and have to start hunting all over again, while my short fuse for reporting into Headquarters kept burning.

Something similar had happened when we piled into Norfolk in a hurry five years earlier. While I went to mandatory in-briefings for my general, also just reporting on board at the Atlantic Command, my wife set out to find us a house. At the end of the first day, I had something of a handle on my new job and she had located a nice rental property. Clearly, she had a solid track record in this business.

I was beginning to talk myself into this sight-unseen deal. Then, the clinching argument rolled in. The biggest problem in buying a house is finding one that appeals to both spouses. Unless some horrible hidden flaw was there to offset the great location, the dual-spouse approval problem was already solved. What the hell—go for it!

I keyed the radio's handset. "Tell her it's okay."

That one short radio call had turned everything upside down. Up to that point, it was relatively easy to stay focused on Lam Son 719 and its aftermath. Now other things were creeping into the picture, such as moving my family from Norfolk to Washington and going into the biggest debt of my life in a matter of weeks. Outprocessing was a blur, and my departure from Saigon's Tan Son Nhut airport was quite unlike my arrival. It was in the middle of the morning, rather than the middle of the night. There were fewer Americans in the terminal—and just about all of them were going home, with no stunned newcomers to tease. For all these folks—and for most of Saigon, it seemed—the war was over, no matter what was going on up north.

Back at Headquarters, I soon discovered that Maj. George Rivers, now serving in the Marine Corps Command Center, was keeping close tabs on the Vietnamese Marines and the co-vans. There were a lot of former advisors around town, and a couple of months after I got back I went to my first annual meeting and party of the Marine Advisors Association, at the Lazy Susan Inn near Woodbridge, Virginia, halfway between Washington, D.C., and Quantico. This well-attended, exuberant affair and the next three that followed were a heady mixture of backslapping, sea stories, debriefing of the latest returnees from the Marine Advisory Unit, and cheers for the newest advisors on their way out to Saigon. To a man, the co-vans in attendance treasured their association with the Vietnamese Marines. They were a special group, with very special memories and strong feelings about the way the war seemed to be winding down. It appeared that the United States was preparing to pull the plug on a nation of seventeen million that it once had committed itself to save.

At the end of March, 1972—almost a year to the day of the wrap-up of Lam Son 719—the North Vietnamese struck southward again in a multi-division attack that soon became known as the Easter Offensive. In due course, the NVA forces ran into a deadly meat-grinder in the Central Highlands, but along the coastal plain it was a different matter entirely, at least at the outset. More than twenty thousand NVA troops, backed by long-range artillery and two hundred tanks, struck across the DMZ, with an axis of advance southward along Route 1. George Rivers's situation map painted a gloomy picture, and accurate and encouraging updates were slow in coming from Vietnam.

After the first day or two, it appeared that the NVA might drive down the coast to Hue City and beyond. There didn't seem to be much in their way, as outgunned South Vietnamese units scrambled to establish a defensive line that could hold, anywhere. If the North Vietnamese maintained their momentum and drove south far enough to threaten Da Nang, the entire country might fall, possibly in a matter of weeks. Once a military rout gains momentum, it becomes difficult to slow down, much less to halt or reverse. The mood around Headquarters was gloomy, as it was at the Pentagon, where intelligence officers were preparing to brief the Army Chief of Staff and former MACV commander, Gen. William Westmoreland, of impending catastrophe.

Then a miracle occurred.

The coastal thrust of the North Vietnamese had been halted at the Cua Viet River, just below the DMZ. The bridge across the Cua Viet at Dong Ha had been cut, and its southernmost span dropped into the river, thanks to Capt. John Ripley, USMC, senior advisor to the Third Battalion. Ripley had spent some three hours under direct fire rigging five hundred pounds of demolitions in the bridge's underside of long girders. Then, with a time fuse already burning, he made one more trip under the bridge, hand-over-hand along the girders, with heavy NVA fire ricocheting all around him, to increase the chances for destruction by rigging a backup electrical fuse.

When the bridge went up, the stalled column of NVA tanks (Soviet-built T-54s) received heavy punishment from U.S. destroyers on the Navy's offshore gun line, called in by Ripley. And when some of the T-54s turned right and began to move inland along the north bank of the Cua Viet, searching for alternate crossing sites, Ripley called in even more devastating naval gunfire on them. Savage fighting continued for days as the NVA eventually found other ways across the Cua Viet and encircled the embattled defenders of Dong Ha.

By the time Ripley and the remnants of the Third Battalion and the ARVN tank battalion—who fought as infantry after their tanks were either destroyed or abandoned for lack of gasoline or ammunition—broke clear of the encirclement, a strong defensive line had been established along the My Chanh River, just south of Quang Tri City. The line held, and the North Vietnamese never got to Hue, at least not this time. The 1972 Easter Offensive sputtered and ground to a halt.

A few weeks later, the South Vietnamese Marines, supported by U.S. helicopters and amphibian tractors, recaptured what was left of Quang Tri City, thus denying the North Vietnamese even the ability to claim control of this northernmost province of South Vietnam. NVA General Vo Nguyen Giap, the architect of the earlier war-ending defeat of the French at Dien Bien Phu, had failed to repeat his earlier success in 1972 and was removed from office quietly by the North Vietnamese Politburo.

It was widely accepted both in the United States and in South Vietnam that Ripley's heroic action at the Dong Ha bridge had bought South Vietnam some valuable time—how much was anyone's guess. Attempts to use this time wisely to strengthen South Vietnam's ability to defend itself, however, were undercut by the precipitate, self-righteous withdrawal of U.S. support that culminated in a refusal by Congress to provide South Vietnam with emergency ammunition during the next big NVA offensive in the spring of 1975. It was a final act of betrayal that a millennium from now may well be regarded as our *least* fine hour.

The three-pronged NVA offensive of 1975 met pockets of stiff resistance, but this time, the Northerners did not have to contend with the punishing U.S. naval gunfire and air support that had thinned their ranks three years earlier. And the only U.S. advisors left in country were technical support folks back in Saigon. None were in the field any more.

In time, the NVA momentum prevailed and the rout was on. By the end of April, some of those T-54 tanks were parked on the lawn of the Presidential Palace in Saigon.

It was over. An almost obscene wave of relief swept over America, but among former co-vans it was the start of a grieving process, one begun in disbelief, quickly moving into rage and sorrow.

The 1975 gathering of the Marine Advisors Association was bloody awful. It would be tempting, but too kind, to compare it with a wake. Real wakes have their upbeat moments, recalling the joyous moments in the life of the deceased. This gathering had none of that. It was morose and belligerent, a real bummer. The mood was intensified by early reports from Vietnam, all bad. According to some second-and third-hand reports, as many as five Vietnamese Marine battalion commanders had died by their own hand, rather than submit to capture by the North Vietnamese. Still more Vietnamese Marines—including my counterpart, Laughing Larry Luong—had died, according to reports, when a barge overturned in Da Nang harbor while carrying Marines to shipping offshore. It was an unmitigated disaster, which no future gathering of Marine advisors could ignore.

For a decade or so, there were no significant gatherings of Marine advisors. The pain was too great.

Thirteen years after his gallant stand in the 1972 Easter Offensive, Col. John Ripley was honored by his fellow 1962 Naval Academy graduates, who had commissioned a diorama depicting his heroism at the bridge, to be placed just outside the entrance to the Academy's Memorial Hall, the Holiest of Holies. This was doubly notable, because John Ripley was not only thus enshrined while he still was alive, but also while he still was on active duty—something unprecedented in the long history of the Academy, dating back to 1845. The Naval Academy Class of 1962, whose graduates arrived in the operational forces as pilots and company-grade ground combat leaders just in time for Vietnam, suffered a record total of killed, wounded, and missing in action. And they wanted co-van Ripley to carry their proud banner of service, in a perpetual setting.

Five years later, Iraq overran Kuwait, and in the ensuing battles of Desert Shield and Desert Storm former co-vans played a key role. It was no accident that former advisors commanded the Marine Expeditionary Force on scene and the MEF afloat just offshore, as well as the two Marine Corps divisions and the major logistical support agency in the area, among many other key players. While many of their contemporaries were easing out of the shoulder straps of their heavy packs, these noteworthy co-vans kept moving toward the sound of the guns, carrying just enough food and a lot of ammunition.

The co-van tradition still was alive.

Not long after Desert Storm, the Vietnamese Marines decided to have a reunion and a party to beat all parties. I got a heads-up call from Col. Don Price, one of the co-vans on the line during the 1972 Easter Offensive. The party would be at a big Vietnamese restaurant in the Seven Corners area of Washington's Virginia suburbs. Vietnamese Marines were coming in from all parts of the country to attend.

"By the way," Don added, "your buddy Luong will be there."

"But he's dead. . . ."

"Dead or alive, The Laugher is going to be there. General Khang ordered him to show up."

My mind was in a pleasant turmoil. Luong got out! Probably living in one of those Vietnamese neighborhoods out in California, eating grapes and getting fat. But why didn't anybody know that earlier?

On the night of the party, I arrived early. Don Price was at the sign-in table.

"Yeah—he's right over there, in a tiger suit. He looks like hell. Just got out of a re-education camp, after seventeen years."

Re-education camp! A typical communist bullshit term for a concentration camp for political prisoners. Luong, who had moved from the G-3 assignment to become a brigade commander by 1975, was one of the six most senior and most powerful Vietnamese Marine officers, maybe the biggest catch those bastards could get their hands on. Seventeen years—first grade all the way through college, with a year of graduate work thrown in. They would need every bit of that to re-educate Luong, and that still might not be enough time for them to get the job done. Luong was one tough man.

But even with Don's warning, I was unprepared for what I saw next. Luong was rail thin, almost emaciated. He had lost his teeth, and the absence of fullness around his mouth made his cheekbones stand out dramatically, giving him a hawk-like appearance. His hair had turned totally white, with not even a hint of gray left, and was set off even more by his deeply tanned skin. Luong had been rather light-skinned, with black hair, so his appearance had the startling effect of presenting a photographic negative of his former self, with light and dark areas reversed.

And oh, how he had aged. The last time I saw him, he had just turned forty-one, and looked more like a thirty-year-old man. That evening, he looked like someone in his mid-seventies, even though he was at least ten years younger. All in all, he resembled an Apache chieftain from our Old West, carved from a block of dark mahogany wood. All except for the eyes. Instead of the fierce defiance of a hawk or chieftain, Luong's eyes showed sadness and a reluctance to engage. It was clear that he'd rather watch the festivities than whoop it up with his brothers-in-arms. Small wonder that General Khang had to order him to attend.

I was reluctant to ask him to dwell on bad memories, by inquiring about his treatment at the hands of his captors, but I did learn that he had just been released a few months earlier. He had joined his family in Richmond, Virginia, where they had settled in the early 1980s after managing to leave Vietnam. In general, I could understand his somber mood, but this was something that went deeper than even the searing experience of his captivity.

It was a glorious evening. Vietnamese Marines kept streaming into the restaurant, some straight from the airport, carrying their luggage with them. And co-vans had come in from all parts of the country, as well, so a spirit of warmth and reunion prevailed as we dined on such delicacies as fish lips soup and heard a parade of speakers, Vietnamese and American, praise the strong bonds that still existed between the Vietnamese and their co-vans. A highlight of the evening was the presentation of Bronze Star Medals to two Vietnamese officers who had not been able to receive them before their capture and seventeen-year incarceration in re-education camps.

As the evening rolled on and the volume of excited chatter kept increasing, something happened at the next table that gave me a sudden flash of insight into Luong's emotional state.

The teenage son of a Vietnamese officer, who looked very much as his father had twenty years earlier, stopped by to pick up a set of car keys. The youngster and his date, dressed for an evening on the town in Dad's car, barely concealed their impatience as Dad introduced them to his table mates. Although they were outwardly deferential to their elders, in true Vietnamese fashion, the looks the young couple exchanged with each other from time to time told me that they had been thoroughly Americanized. Any parent of teenagers has, at one time or another, seen The Look—thinly veiled superiority and insolence that appears in flashes when the young one is forced to acknowledge or deal with his mentally defective, clueless elders. And that was what Luong was facing. He was trying to find his way in a new land, with English skills rusted over seventeen years, while trying to regain control of a household that had gone on without him, headed by his wife. His children had a ten-year start on becoming Americanized, in ways both good and bad. I didn't envy him.

But Luong was a survivor, and he would prevail here, too. Deep inside, I knew he would. And as the evening wore on, he began to lighten up, as though he were trying to justify my faith in his ability to rebound. At one point, a very powerful woman singer took the stage microphone and began to do violence to our eardrums. Luong and I looked at each other and said the magic word simultaneously: *Be-năm mười hai* (five times ten plus two).

It was just like being back at the Bong Lai. The B-52 was singing once again.

As the evening wrapped up, a co-van finally broached the big question to one of the Bronze Star recipients:

"What did you really *do* in those re-education camps?"

"Well—we worked. We got up at sunrise and worked all day planting rice, building roads, or whatever hard labor they could find for us. Then every couple of weeks they would haul us off to an auditorium somewhere and tell us about how great communism is. . . ."

He paused for a moment, thinking about all those lost years in his life. Then he suddenly brightened, and finished with a big smile:

"But they could never get to us—we're *Marines!*

The author, during the first week *(above)* and six months into his 1970–71 tour as a co-van.

About the Author

John Grider Miller is the managing editor of the Naval Institute's *Proceedings* and *Naval History* magazines. A 1957 graduate of Yale University and retired Marine Corps colonel, he has seen extensive infantry service, including two tours of duty in Vietnam as a rifle company commander and an advisor to the South Vietnamese Marine Corps. He has also served as deputy director of Marine Corps history and principal speechwriter for three Commandants.

In 1985 the Naval Institute Press published his first book, *The Battle to Save the Houston,* which is being republished this year in the Bluejacket Books series. His second book, *The Bridge at Dong Ha,* followed in 1989, with its Bluejacket Books edition appearing in 1996. It brought Miller the 1989 Gen. Wallace M. Greene, Jr. Book Award from the Marine Corps Historical Foundation. He was named the Naval Institute's Book Author of the Year in 1990, and received the lifetime Distinguished Service Award from the Marine Corps Heritage Foundation in 1998.

The Naval Institute Press is the book-publishing arm of the U.S. Naval Institute, a private, nonprofit, membership society for sea service professionals and others who share an interest in naval and maritime affairs. Established in 1873 at the U.S. Naval Academy in Annapolis, Maryland, where its offices remain today, the Naval Institute has members worldwide.

Members of the Naval Institute support the education programs of the society and receive the influential monthly magazine *Proceedings* and discounts on fine nautical prints and on ship and aircraft photos. They also have access to the transcripts of the Institute's Oral History Program and get discounted admission to any of the Institute-sponsored seminars offered around the country.

The Naval Institute also publishes *Naval History* magazine. This colorful bimonthly is filled with entertaining and thought-provoking articles, first-person reminiscences, and dramatic art and photography. Members receive a discount on *Naval History* subscriptions.

The Naval Institute's book-publishing program, begun in 1898 with basic guides to naval practices, has broadened its scope in recent years to include books of more general interest. Now the Naval Institute Press publishes about one hundred titles each year, ranging from how-to books on boating and navigation to battle histories, biographies, ship and aircraft guides, and novels. Institute members receive discounts of 20 to 50 percent on the Press's more than eight hundred books in print.

Full-time students are eligible for special half-price membership rates. Life memberships are also available.

For a free catalog describing Naval Institute Press books currently available, and for further information about subscribing to *Naval History* magazine or about joining the U.S. Naval Institute, please write to:

Membership Department
U.S. Naval Institute
291 Wood Road
Annapolis, MD 21402-5034
Telephone: (800) 233-8764
Fax: (410) 269-7940
Web address: www.usni.org

Please remember that this is a library book,
and that it belongs only temporarily to each
person who uses it. Be considerate. Do
not write in this, or any, library book.

DATE DUE
